"If you've ever bounced along to TLC's 'Scrubs' in your car on a girls' night out, acted out a three-act play in your head to My Chemical Romance's 'The Black Parade,' or swooned to Barry Manilow's 'Could It Be Magic,' and wondered, *How* did *these anthemic songs come to be*?—join the club! Steve Baltin so brilliantly takes you deep into an insightful journey of these songs from inception to recording and beyond. . . .

"So many fascinating artists and songs that are woven into the soundtrack of our lives in a new and unique way that will leave you hungry for a next edition. This book resonates with me as a songwriter, but more importantly, it hits home for the music fan that lives in all of us!"

—DEBORAH GIBSON

STEVE BALTIN

Anthems We Love

29 ICONIC ARTISTS ON THE
SONGS THAT SHAPED OUR LIVES

HARPER HORIZON

Published by Harper Horizon, an imprint of HarperCollins Focus LLC.

Book design by Aubrey Khan, Neuwirth & Associates, Inc.

ISBN 978-0-7852-9053-7 (eBook)
ISBN 978-0-7852-9052-0 (HC)

Library of Congress Control Number: 2022934021

Printed in the United States of America
22 23 24 25 26 LSC 10 9 8 7 6 5 4 3 2 1

Dedicated to Sierra, my best friend;

Phyllis Baltin, my mom; Ben Jacobs, my cousin;

Duder, and all the other souls of the departed

who I wish were here to see this book.

CONTENTS

✦

FOREWORD

✦

I have a theory.

Most great anthems are mistakes. It seems that every time a songwriter, or a band, tries to create a song for *everybody*, they often please nobody. The same often goes for movies or politicians, but our subject here is music. The quest to create a global delight usually dies quickly on the battlefield of commerce and empty purpose. They usually miss the most important element: a song has to first mean something to *one* person before it can mean something to everybody. But I could be wrong. I've needed a definitive piece of detective work to get to the bottom of this theory. And now, just in time, comes this wonderful book.

Steve Baltin is the man for this job. Baltin more than knows music—he *feels* music. His journey in writing this book finds him shining a light into all the nooks and crannies of what goes into the creation of an anthem. To watch Baltin conduct an interview is to experience a master class in the art of summoning secrets and untold stories. In a world where most interviewers are waiting to talk, he knows how to listen. On a recent press tour with the charming and sometimes prickly David Crosby, about whom I'd produced a documentary, I watched Baltin effortlessly engage Crosby in the best conversation of our tour. Why? Because Baltin makes it personal. He's not digging for stories for an audience. He's digging for truths for himself, and make no mistake: Baltin *loves* music.

Which brings us to this fine subject, anthems.

As the rock generation ages past retirement, fewer and fewer of the pioneering musicians, the true titans of the genre, are around to share their stories. Some never *have* shared their secrets. Steve Baltin's assignment in writing this book was simple but enormously tough. In some cases, he's asking for new revelations about some of the most listened-to compositions and records of our time. Often, the most famous songs are the least interesting for an artist to talk about. It can be a Herculean task to pull a fresh anecdote from a seventy-five-year-old artist talking about a fifty-year-old song. Baltin scales these hurdles effortlessly, with a fan's devotion and a clear-eyed reporter's unerring sense of detail. The result is Baltin's magic trick. Suddenly the stories all ring with freshness, and these songs feel new again. Interestingly, many of the anthems examined within were not immediately heralded. Reading Baltin's take on "God Only Knows," from the Beach Boys' seminal *Pet Sounds*, it's clear that a masterpiece is often something that needs to brew over time. Paul Stanley found that his "surefire" KISS anthem "Rock and Roll All Nite" had to wait for a subsequent live album to be fully appreciated. Sometimes a song can be so original it's initially even off-putting. Don McLean remembers performing "American Pie" early on, opening for Laura Nyro, and the audience found the song baffling. Janis Ian's "At Seventeen" wasn't an instant favorite either.

Or there is a song like the Temptations' "My Girl," which proved Motown founder Berry Gordy's dictum: a hit is built from simplicity and truth. Carly Simon wrote "Anticipation" because she was bored and waiting for her date to arrive. Graham Nash scored his biggest hit with a bare-bones song about domestic love, "Our House." A love song for then flame Joni Mitchell, Nash's anthem grew from a song almost *too* simple for him. Over fifty years, he's seen his song travel from exalted worldwide acclaim to a near albatross to the point where today, Nash has rekindled his own love affair with the song. Poignantly, he tells Baltin that when he now performs "Our House," he feels compelled to experience it with all its original passion, as a gift to his fans. Talk about a full-circle anthem.

Sometimes it's the song these writers least expect to blossom. It's the throwaway that a loved one needs to convince them to finish ("Everybody Wants to Rule the World") or the one that was almost too silly ("Le Freak"). Sometimes it was a simple breakthrough that was hiding in plain sight, such as three words falling together and suddenly sounding like a phrase we'd known forever ("Light My Fire"). And even then, the Doors had to butter up a local DJ with a live club performance before he'd play the song—to instant success.

These are the stories that add new luster to some of our most familiar favorites. *Anthems We Love* is not merely a tale of artistic adventure; it's also a manual for artists and fans alike. There is no formula. Just these inspiring stories of the heart, and Steve Baltin's sparkling portraits of these artists who looked into their souls and often accidentally created indelible songs for all time. Every once in a while, the world claims a little piece of pop poetry and says: "This is it. That's what it feels like to be alive." Here are the definitive origin stories of those rare and cherished songs that live on . . . and on . . . and on.

CAMERON CROWE
November 2021

PROLOGUE

✦

*V*ery rarely does an anthem begin with the ambitious intention to create something for the ages. Sometimes it's a combination of luck, risk, and art colliding in unexpected ways. I had the good fortune to have produced and arranged the hit record that helped propel Quiet Riot and their *Metal Health* album to number one in *Billboard* magazine, the first hard-rock record to do so in music history. When I was in my Los Angeles–based recording studio making "Cum On Feel the Noize," the band (famously reticent to record the song in the first place) and I had no idea that forty years later it would still be considered a rallying call for heavy-metal fun. I still marvel at its trajectory and staying power every time I hear it played or see it featured somewhere. It might not carry the emotional weight we experience with many of the songs featured in this book, but it definitely possesses the traits that make a song an anthem.

I've been producing, arranging records, and writing songs for nearly five decades, starting with Tina Turner as the Acid Queen in the Who's *Tommy* in 1975. Since then I've had the privilege of working with some of the greatest artists of all time, including Stevie Wonder, Little River Band, Cheap Trick, Heart, B.B. King, and Graham Nash, whose "Our House" is included in this book.

I am still at it, currently mentoring twenty-four-year-old UK breaking songwriter-artist Jade Bird and producing the Paramount+ documentary on the impact and influence of Don McLean's "American Pie," another anthem featured in these pages.

It's been an incredible ride with plenty of ups and downs. I've heard the word *no* more times than I can remember. In 1983, twenty-one labels passed on Quiet Riot's *Metal Health* album before I convinced then CBS Records president and CEO Walter Yetnikoff to release it. I had to fund and produce the music video for "Bang Your Head" myself. MTV premiered it at a not-quite-prime-time slot, four o'clock in the morning.

When the record went platinum in sales and then sold millions of copies, all the decision makers at the labels, who initially rejected the music, phoned to effuse how much they loved it. Of course, the truth was that they had hated it and were convinced it would bomb, but they weren't about to admit it. That experience taught me that just because others say no doesn't mean you have to accept it.

✦ ✦ ✦

By the end of 1983, *Metal Health* became the first hard-rock album to hit number one on the Billboard charts. I knew we had something special on our hands but it wasn't until I heard stadium audiences chanting the chorus from the album's "Cum On Feel the Noize" that I realized we had truly connected with the zeitgeist.

Cum on feel the noize
Girls, rock your boys
We'll get wild, wild, wild
Wild, wild, wild

The song, a reimagining of Slade's glam-rock effort, was pure metal rock 'n' roll for the eighties. And a pure anthem for the ages. Decades later, it amazes me that this simple chorus, celebrating youth and anarchy, still matters to millions.

✦ ✦ ✦

It was three years ago when I met journalist Steve Baltin. Steve interviewed me for a *Forbes* article and we struck up a mutual respect and new friendship, which led to the conceptualization and writing of this book. It was this Quiet Riot story that led to his suggestion that we create a book about anthems. We both feel fortunate to have teamed with publisher Andrea Fleck-Nisbet, who shares our vision for the project.

Steve conducted all the interviews with the iconic talent featured on the following pages. His style is conversant and not interrogatory, and you'll feel as if you're sitting with the artists, hearing these stories firsthand. I weigh in on certain songs where we felt my contribution from a direct, firsthand nexus and relationship to the music and the artist might add a little something.

It's through the grace and support of so many people in my life that this book was possible. While playing quarterback growing up, I learned that in football, it takes eleven teammates working together in harmony to score a touchdown. One may cross the goal line with the ball but if the other ten don't do their jobs, nothing good happens. I wasn't a great quarterback but I was *just* smart enough to understand that when I did get into the game, all I had to do was my job: call the right play, get rid of the ball, and move the hell out of the way. In the end, it's all about playing your best game, winning if stars and efforts are aligned—and it doesn't matter how you do it as long it involves teamwork. For the better part of five decades, that's been my MO in business and in life.

After the sobering realization that I was never going to be quarterbacking my hometown Los Angeles Rams to the Super Bowl, I dove fully into my other passion: making music. And at the end of the day, I'm still a quarterback at heart and like I was all those years ago, *just* smart enough to know which play to call, when to get rid of the ball, and how to move the hell out of the way.

SPENCER PROFFER
Los Angeles, 2022

*T*here are two essential ingredients for an anthem. The first is timelessness. An anthem is a song that transcends genres, generations, and eras, to continually reach new fans over the decades.

The second, and more important, is universality. The truly great songwriters have the gift of writing a song that can be penned about the most intimate detail of their life but makes the listener feel like it was written about their own story. And hearing that song takes the listener back to a specific place and time.

Every time I hear Barry Manilow, whose "Could It Be Magic" is one of the twenty-nine songs in this collection, I immediately think of my mother, who passed in 2018, and her love of his music. The same is true of the great Neil Diamond, another of her favorite artists. I remember seeing him at the Forum in LA with my college girlfriend, my mom, and her boyfriend.

When I hear KISS's "Rock and Roll All Nite," I am taken back to my first rock concert. Ten years old at the Forum, sitting next to some guy clearly on drugs. The lights went down for KISS, and the guy, who hadn't moved all night, lifted his head and howled loudly, scaring the crap out of ten-year-old me.

The stories go on and on. I reviewed U2's "One" for the *Washington Square News* while a student at New York University; I traveled on the road with Linkin Park in 2004 for a book, *From the Inside: Linkin Park's Meteora*, hearing "In the End" night after night; and when I hear My Chemical Romance's "Welcome to the Black Parade," I think of Halloween night 2006, seeing them at House of Blues in LA for an AOL concert.

I can attribute a personal story and memory to every one of the twenty-nine songs in this book. And far, far more importantly, so can everybody who loves these songs.

In this book are memories of the Temptations' eternal "My Girl" being played at weddings and birthdays. There are countless women named Sara, after Hall & Oates' "Sara Smile." There are so many teenage parties that come with "Rock and Roll All Nite," Aerosmith's "Walk This Way," the Doors' "Light My Fire," and Linkin Park's "In the End." There are first dates, many of which led to marriage, while listening to Carly Simon's "Anticipation," Janis Ian's "At Seventeen," and Shania Twain's "You're Still the One." There are tears, some of joy and some of sorrow, while listening to the Beach Boys' "God Only Knows," and there are the endless memories of joyous dancing when Earth, Wind & Fire's "September" and CHIC's "Le Freak" are heard.

These are the songs that are played at weddings, funerals, parties, and sporting events, and even when a listener is home alone. These songs are played by grandparents and parents for their kids and grandkids; they are played by older brothers and sisters, babysitters, and friends, introducing these anthems to young generations.

Songs like the Doors' "Light My Fire" and Jefferson Airplane's "White Rabbit" are passed down by teenagers from generation to generation, resonating as loudly, deeply, and profoundly with fourteen-year-olds in 2021 as they did when first released in 1967, known as the Summer of Love.

These are the songs that have been passed down like family heirlooms and family secrets. These are twenty-nine of the greatest songs of all time.

No one is claiming that these are *the* twenty-nine greatest songs of all time. But what we are claiming is that every one of these songs—all twenty-nine, from the first to the last—are iconic and have made a significant and lasting impact on popular culture. Some of these songs have endured more than fifty years. Even the most recent have now lasted for decades.

How have they lasted? How is it that fourteen-year-olds around the world discover "Light My Fire" every year? Whether it is through cover versions, use in movies and TV, or whatever the case might be, every one of these songs has stood the test of time. And as you read through the individual chapters you will see many of the artists, from KISS's Paul Stanley to the Jackson 5's Tito Jackson, talk about the feeling of seeing kids not even born when these songs came out sing their words back to them.

So every song in here has proven to be timeless and transcended its genre and its era. That was the primary criterion used to select these songs. We didn't want hits that defined a certain period. We wanted songs that have lasted and remain relevant today. After that, many things go into assembling a book like this.

The first, obviously, is artist availability. In beginning a project of this size and scope, you start with a wish list of songs and artists, and then it evolves on its own over the course of the book.

If you would have told me when I started reaching out to artists in December 2019 that this would be the final roster of twenty-nine songs and artists, I would not have believed a range this wide and this renowned would be possible.

To have a list that goes from the Temptations and the Beach Boys to U2 and TLC, from the sixties to the aughts, and covers almost all genres in between, is a dream come true for this self-proclaimed music geek. To have a book with the Temptations' Otis Williams, the last living member to have recorded "My Girl"; to have an original chapter penned by the great Tom Waits and his wife, Kathleen Brennan; to have Linda Ronstadt in here; and to have Shania Twain tell stories of Prince and Elton John singing her song is wildly beyond expectations for any music lover.

In these next twenty-nine chapters you will read, in the artists' words, how songs like Bob Marley's "One Love"—as told by his son Stephen—Tears for Fears' "Everybody Wants to Rule the World," TOTO's "Africa," TLC's "No Scrubs," and twenty-five more songs became anthems, how the songs grew from the studios to take their place as part of pop culture lore.

Throughout my career, I have been fortunate to talk to many of the greatest songwriters alive—from Willie Nelson, Neil Young, and Stevie Wonder to Dolly Parton, Stevie Nicks, and Alicia Keys—and they all say the same thing: that once they put a song into the world it is no longer theirs. As soon as a song is released it belongs to the world and all you can do, as an artist, is hope for the best for your baby.

These twenty-nine songs were sent into the world and did the best they could. Every one of them has made a difference in our lives, whether in times of joy or sorrow, of celebration or reflection, or for a milestone or a loss. When you read these stories and think of these songs, you can't help but put your own lifetime of memories into each song. And that's why these are *anthems*.

CHAPTER ONE

THE TEMPTATIONS

✦ "MY GIRL" ✦

&very one of the twenty-nine songs in this book is be-loved and revered for its own unique reasons. Take the Temptations' classic "My Girl," which hit number one on both the Billboard Hot 100 and the Billboard R&B charts in 1965, though it was released in December 1964, and has since been inducted into the Grammy Hall of Fame and the National Recording Registry at the Library of Congress. It is hard to think of a song that elicits more warmth and positive vibes than "My Girl."

The opening line—"I've got sunshine on a cloudy day"—is the perfect metaphor for how the song has made listeners feel for more than half a century. Otis Williams, the last remaining of the five Temptations who were on the original recording, believes it is because everyone can relate to the song's feeling of love.

"I think from the womb to the tomb, most men—ain't going to say all—but most men would like to find a girl that he can refer to as 'My Girl,'" Williams says. "So it is so relative about that song because everybody wants something that they consider 'My Girl.' Smokey [Robinson] wrote a big hit record, which went to number one with Mary Wells with 'My Guy.' Somebody was teasing Smokey, 'Oh man you got a hit on "My Guy," now you're going to do another one about "My Girl"?' Sure enough, Smokey did it, went to number one, turned out to be a hit."

The song, which was the first Temptations track to feature the legendary David Ruffin on lead vocals, was in part inspired by Ruffin's smooth vocals, as Williams remembers it.

"Let me tell you how that song came about. Smokey came to see us at a very popular club in Detroit called Twenty Grand. So he saw the show and said to us—this is the original chapter [of the Temptations]—'You guys are fantastic.' He was giving us accolades or whatever," Williams says. "Then Smokey stopped and he looked at David; he said, 'I got a song for you.' So us being young, cocky, we said, 'Man, bring it on.' And we sang it that night."

The close camaraderie of the Motown acts during that midsixties period made it natural for the song to grow quickly from Robinson's writing to the classic the Temps recorded, as they were working together frequently on the road.

"We had to close at the Twenty Grand and with the Miracles and the Temps who were appearing in New York City at the Apollo Theater. Smokey would rehearse us in between shows at the Apollo. So we did the Apollo, came back to Detroit, went in the studio, and basically put the voices on the track of 'My Girl,'" Williams says. "But I have always said, aside from 'My Girl' being such a great song, when Paul Riser added the strings and horns I started hearing with those beautiful strings and the arrangement of the song it took on a whole other light."

Once Williams heard the combination of Riser's arrangement, Ruffin's lead vocals, and Robinson's songwriting, he knew they had crafted something special. Though he admits he had no idea he would still be talking about the song nearly sixty years later.

"Smokey was in the control room being a producer. And I came in, I said, 'Smokey, I don't know how big a record this is going to become. But I got a feeling that this is going to be a huge record,'" he says.

Indeed it was. "'My Girl' was released December 21, 1964. February 1965 the Temps were at the Apollo Theater. We were number one, sold over a million copies," he recalls. "Berry [Gordy] sent us a telegram congratulating us. The Supremes sent us a telegram congratulating us. The theater sent us a telegram congratulating us on 'My Girl' being such a hit. And I often think, 'Wow, it started from "I got a song for you."' To see it come from that."

The song became an immediate hit, reaching number one January 16, 1965, less than a month after it was released as a single December 21, 1964. So although Williams remembers rehearsing the song at the Apollo, the quintet had actually been performing the song for some time before the Apollo show.

"We had been doing it elsewhere before we came to the Apollo because, naturally promotion, you're going to do it. And then we were doing some one-nighters," he says. "But I guess by the time we got to the Apollo, evidently at the time it sold one million copies and reached number one."

As the band was performing the song on the road, Williams saw immediately how audiences responded to the song's good vibrations and message of love. "Back at that time it was taking on such a life of its own, once they started hearing that boom-boom-boom, the ladies in particular were going crazy," he says. "So it was just a wonderful event everywhere we'd go until we got the Apollo and it had reached number one. It was just one of those songs that they fell in love with instantaneously, even before we got to the Apollo. By the time we got to the Apollo and Berry sent us the telegram it was number one, the song was zippity-do-dah gone, it was gone. We were doing TV shows, we were even doing TV shows as a promotion before we got to the Apollo for it to become number one because Motown was sending us around to radio stations and doing record hops and things of that nature. And the fervor was great even then before it became number one. So all that expedited it to become a huge record."

Over time, the world's love of the song has not only never faded, as Williams learned the hard way when they took it out of the set at one point, but it has grown almost exponentially in the last fifty years.

"Even today, we did it up there in Utah, and when they heard the dah-dah-dah, dah-dah-dah, people started standing up like trees growing from the ground. Now we're talking about 1964, went number one in 1965, here we are in 2021, so it's been a continuous appreciation and love for that song. It's just ongoing," he says. "We took it out because we thought it had peaked, which it had. We thought, *They don't care about that. They want to hear that song.* They were calling us everything except the child of God. And we will never, ever take 'My Girl' out of the lineup. So it's a song that continue to be a part of who we are going on up."

Like all of the songs in this collection, "My Girl" has taken on additional life through massive popularity in popular culture and with other artists. It has been covered over two hundred times by some of the greatest artists of all time: Otis Redding, Stevie Wonder, the Rolling Stones, Al Green, Diana Ross and the Supremes with the Temptations, Michael Jackson, Dolly Parton, Phil Collins, Michael Bolton, and many more. It has even been covered by two other artists in this collection, Hall & Oates and Barry Manilow with Melissa Manchester.

Williams is flattered every time an artist does the song, especially by the top-tier talent that have lent their voices and names to "My Girl."

"Each artist that you mentioned, they did it the way they sing a song. And I have a great appreciation for it, because first and foremost, they didn't have to do it. So when they wanna do it, Dolly Parton, Otis Redding, I've heard them and the others. So I'm appreciative for whatever artists wanna do one of our songs in their own rendition," he says. "That's who they are, that's what made them the way they are. Think about Rod Stewart. Rod Stewart is such a big, wonderful Temptations fan. He's been to see us a few times. So I take each of those as a wonderful compliment because first and foremost they don't have to do that. They are stars in their own right. So to make that kind of acknowledgment about when they do one of our songs and what have you? I love it."

The song's popularity with other artists is mirrored by its endless appeal to Hollywood. It is one of only a few songs to directly inspire a film's title. And if there were any doubt about the influence of the Temptations song on the sweet, 1991 box-office hit of the same name, that was erased when the song played over the final credits of the Anna Chlumsky and Macaulay Culkin movie.

My Girl, which grossed over $120 million worldwide, is the only work to share a title with the Temps song, but hardly the only movie or TV show to prominently feature the song. It has appeared in the TV series *New Girl*, *Hawaii Five-O*, *So You Think You Can Dance*, *Cold Case*, *Full House*, the original version of *The Wonder Years*, *Saturday Night Live*, and more, be it reality TV, dramas, sitcoms, or variety shows. It feels like "My Girl" goes back as far as TV itself (not quite, but close).

As you would expect, the list of movies to feature "My Girl" is just as long and diverse, from the 1984 feel-good Best Picture Oscar nominee *The Big Chill* to 2006 Best Picture Oscar nominee Steven Spielberg's *Munich*. It's also been part of the 2015 family comedy *Daddy's Home*, starring Mark Wahlberg and Will Ferrell; science fiction film *Hardcore Henry*; the hilarious music comedy *Walk Hard: The Dewey Cox Story*, with John C. Reilly; the sports-themed family movie *The Game Plan*, starring Dwayne "The Rock" Johnson; and *Hollywood Homicide*, an action comedy with Harrison Ford and Josh Hartnett.

Of the dozens of uses of "My Girl," Williams doesn't play favorites, saying they all have meaning to him. "I love them all 'cause you never would expect to be acknowledged in those kinds of films and plays and shows and what have you. So I can't say one of those. Each one brings joy to me and my heart," he says. "To see the people in like *The Big Chill*, how they reacted to 'My Girl,' and the others. I say, 'Wow.' Case in point, Spike Lee just made a movie that came out, *Da 5 Bloods*. He based that on each one of the original Temps. I've had such a storied career. So I can't have one stand out and not the others because each one, they got an importance in my life and to the Temptations that are equal to all the rest."

But what is it about "My Girl" that allows the song to fit into comedies, period dramas, action or family films, and more? It's simple. It's the feelings it evokes of nostalgia, of love, of protection, of longing, and most importantly, of family.

Although "My Girl" was clearly written originally as a love song, it has become an anthem for fathers and daughters the world over in the last fifty-plus years. Williams cannot count how many times he and the group have been asked to sing it at weddings for father-daughter dances.

"We've been at shows where the daughter would get married. And they would request, could they come up onstage and sing 'My Girl'? Or private parties, the father and his daughter would get on the floor and dance to us singing 'My Girl.' We've had all forms of entertainment concerning 'My Girl,'" he says. "They want to get on the stage. We do everything else in our repertoire, but when it came to 'My Girl,' they would love to come out and sing 'My Girl' with you. We make an exception. Say, 'Oh yeah, no problem. Getting married, yeah, no problem.' They'd come on up there and do it. So we've had that and we still have that. Someone called and asked us the other day, 'A father and daughter would like to know if they could come up.' We'll do it all the time, do 'My Girl.' So we get all kind of reasons of why they would like to come out onstage with us. To do 'My Girl' or stand there while we do 'My Girl.' The father, the daughter dance to 'My Girl.' It has been different ways."

There is one story of family that stands out the most to Williams, one involving fan mail he got over a decade ago. "So this one particular fan mail, I was sat down, and I ended up reading it. This is the daughter [about] her mother. She said, 'Mr. Williams, would you please call my mother? I'm a fan and she's a fan. So my mother would like to talk to you,'" he recalls. "So I said, 'Okay.' So I'm dialing the number and I say, 'Yeah, this is Otis Williams, I'm calling because you asked me to give you a call?' The daughter said, 'Hold on, Mr. Williams, let me get my mother.' The mother came on the phone and the first thing that came out of her mouth was, 'I asked God not to take me until I talked to Otis Williams.' I sat there and said, 'Oh my goodness.' And she ran down to me the importance of the Temptations and our music and Motown. And when I just sat there and I listened. And now I'm sitting there with my beer with tears running down my eyes. And when she says, 'My God, you can take me. I have talked to Otis Williams,' I have never, ever had anybody who said that to me. The power of music. The power of Motown. The power of the Temptations and 'My Girl.' Don't get any heavier than that. When you ask God, 'Hold up, hold up—before you take me I need to talk to Otis.' I never will forget that."

This was the most personal story he had ever experienced, but over the last six decades he has heard too many stories of the meaning of the Temptations' music to recount.

"I've been told, aside from that, I've had fans to tell me, somebody from their family, 'Would you please put a Temptations album or record in my coffin?' And I say 'No, no, no, no,'" he says. "And they say, 'No, Otis, I'm telling you. They wanted a Temptations album with them in their final resting place.' It don't get any heavier than that. When they take our music to their final resting place? Can't top that. That's it, that's the coup de grâce."

Though he has been part of the Temptations more than fifty years, he understands those fans whose lives have been so impacted by the Temptations they want to take the music with them for eternity. Williams is a Temptations fan himself.

"I'm a big Temptations fan. When I listen to it, be it accidental or on purpose, I'll listen and say, 'Man we have such a storied life career.' And 'Papa Was a Rollin' Stone.' Man, public don't know it almost didn't get to be made. 'Ball of Confusion,' [written in] 1968, still very relevant, here it is 2021. And I would sit and listen to that, I'd say, 'Man, the history of our songs.' It's just mind-boggling. Even to me and I've been every step of the way," he says. "But when I go back, I look in my rearview mirror of life and I am so impressed and in awe of our catalog, how the world still loves the Temps, in spite of losing the original guys.

They still love the Temptations. Most cases when you lose a Da-vid Ruffin that would be the end. And Dennis Edwards . . . I live and am still living a very storied life as far as being in the Temp-tations. As far as representing music and Motown and what we are all known for. I'm just blown away still and I've been in it from day one, signed a contract in March of 1961, which I still have hanging up in one of my rooms. So little did I imagine that I would have such a career with all the music and the success, my life story being a miniseries. And from a miniseries to a Broadway hit. So I look back at it. It was just something that God gave me."

Of course the Temps have so many hits. As he mentioned, "Papa Was A Rollin' Stone" and "Ball of Confusion," but also "Just My Imagination," "Ain't Too Proud to Beg," "The Way You Do the Things You Do," and so many more.

But Williams is well aware that no song has captured the pub-lic's imagination the way "My Girl" has. It has stood the test of time for more than half a century, and there is little doubt that the song's popularity will continue. And he can tell you why the song has endured and will endure for so long.

"I can tell you, it's simple and easy: it's a great song. 'My Girl,' when you break it down, is not complicated. The melody is so [easy], when I saw a little three-, four-year-old kid doing that. So it's easy. Those are the real songs that ultimately become hit re-cords. When the melody is easy enough that a child can remem-ber. And sing along with it. It don't have to get complicated with a whole lot of fancy music and all that. No. The song itself has got to have all the trademarks of being a great song. And that's what happened with 'My Girl,'" he says. "It's very simple to sing, the arrangement. And when Paul Riser added the strings, I said, 'Oh my God, that is beautiful, beautiful.' But the song itself, even with all the beautiful casing around it, the song itself had the melody, the lyrics. The lyrics hit home, like I said, from the womb to the tomb, I would think most men would like to have a woman where he can say, that's my girl. So it's very simple. K-I-S-S: keep it simple, stupid. That's what makes great hits."

CHAPTER TWO

THE BEACH BOYS

+ "GOD ONLY KNOWS" +

Whats the saying? "The more things change, the more they stay the same." That is certainly true of the timelessness of the Beach Boys' "God Only Knows." Reflecting on when people first heard the song in 1966, Brian Wilson says today, "People cried when they heard it."

More than fifty years later the song is still moving people, especially musicians, to tears. Glass Animals' front man Dave Bayley, who was born more than two decades after the song was released, said in a *Forbes* interview, "The song that's really haunted me is 'God Only Knows' because that just keeps taking on new meanings as you go through life. I often ask people if the world was going to end, what three songs would you listen to. I change my three songs all the time, but 'God Only Knows' is on there most often."[1]

The impact "God Only Knows" has had on Wilson's fellow musicians is well-documented through history. Most famously, a gentleman by the name of Paul McCartney, who knows a thing or two about songwriting, is quoted as calling it "the greatest song ever written."

McCartney, who performed the song with Wilson in 2002 at the Adopt-A-Minefield Benefit Gala, told Radio 1 in 2007: "'God Only Knows' is one of the few songs that reduces me to tears every time I hear it. It's really just a love song, but it's brilliantly done. It shows the genius of Brian. I've actually performed it with him and I'm afraid to say that during the sound check I broke down. It was just too much to stand there singing this song that does my head in, and to stand there singing it with Brian."[2]

McCartney might be the most famous songwriter to advocate for "God Only Knows" as the greatest pop song ever. But he is hardly alone, as several other legends have also sung the song's praises.

Bono, front man of Rock & Roll Hall of Famer U2, said during Wilson's 2006 UK Music Hall of Fame induction that the song's strings are "fact and proof of angels."[3]

The Who's Pete Townshend said in a quote that appears on Brian Wilson's website, "'God Only Knows' is simple and elegant and was stunning when it first appeared; it still sounds perfect."[4]

And Barry Gibb, another dual member, like McCartney, of both the Rock & Roll Hall of Fame and Songwriters Hall of Fame, also calls it one of his favorite songs, saying in a post on Wilson's website that it "blew the top of my head off! . . . My first thought was, 'Oh, dear, I'm wasting my time, how can I ever compete with that?' We've been competing with that ever since."[5]

Then there are the countless artists who have covered the song over the years. The song has been covered more than two hundred times, by artists as wildly diverse as David Bowie, Elton

John, the Chicks' Natalie Maines, the Flaming Lips, Bryan Adams, Brandi Carlile, hard-rock heroes Avenged Sevenfold, Olivia Newton-John, Andy Williams, R.E.M.'s Michael Stipe, Taylor Swift, and many more.

There are two versions, though, that stand out most for Wilson. The first is the cover Lyle Lovett did when Wilson was feted at the Kennedy Center Honors in 2007, of which Wilson says now, "I just remember I really liked it." And the second is the all-star rendition Wilson was a part of to launch BBC Music in 2014. That interpretation featured Wilson, Stevie Wonder, Dave Grohl, Florence Welch, Chris Martin, Kylie Minogue, Pharrell Williams, Sam Smith, Lorde, and more.

It's fitting the song would be used for such a special occasion in the UK. Both Al Jardine, who played with Wilson in the Beach Boys and on Wilson's recent solo tours, and Wilson recall London in particular picking up on *Pet Sounds* and "God Only Knows" before the rest of the world.

"At the time that kind of recognition came primarily from the British fans," Jardine says in his own interview for this book.

When Wilson recalls the early days of playing the song live, he also remembers UK fans giving the song the best response. "People would cheer," he says, "especially in London."

Reflecting on it now, Jardine recalls the song, though exceptional, being one of many the band had to learn for the stage. So there wasn't necessarily time to digest what Wilson had done with this particular song.

"When we came home from our tour we were hit with everything, not just one song. Brian had all of *Pet Sounds* pretty much ready to go, all the vocals, so we were hit with like a landslide of sorts of work. So no one particular song stood out except for what I sang or sang lead on for instance. The rest was just a massive amount of vocalizations for not only *Pet Sounds*, but *Smile*, as we were doing both projects at the same time. So it was kind of a blur to be honest with you. So I don't remember it particularly being any more wonderful than the rest," he says, laughing. "We had a lot of work, a lot of material to cover, that we'd never even heard before. We were basically helping to fill out the most important element, being the vocals. So that's what you got, you got a challenge. And then to perform them live was a whole other challenge. How do you do it live? Fortunately it was pretty simple production, 'God Only Knows,' compared to the rest of the album. That was kind of nice because Carl [Wilson]'s vocal stood out. And we didn't need a whole lot of voices onstage to perform. It was pretty straightforward so that helped."

The song was an immediate success in the live sets, even if the song's beauty didn't lend itself to a crowd rocking out the way they would to "California Girls" or "Surfing USA."

"The shows were tailored to dovetail into one another and part of the show was more down, more of a quiet section," Jardine says. "That's always a nice place to be in the set because it's such a beautiful song and Carl does it so well. It was a feature in the set, but we didn't expect a huge amount of crowd response. It was more oohs and aahs from the audience. From our end we were just supporting Carl really. The song itself, when it got to be a crowd favorite, it's more respectful. It just fits that sequence in our set and it worked."

Of course, if the audience had been nothing but musicians they would have likely rushed the stage during "God Only Knows." How revered is "God Only Knows" in the musical community? Think about this: beyond the cover versions mentioned above, it might be the only song in history covered by Neil Diamond, David Bowie, and Elton John, all three in the Songwriters Hall of Fame and Rock & Roll Hall of Fame. So when a song has been covered by that very different trio and hailed by McCartney and Gibb and others, it is safe to say "God Only Knows" is a songwriter's song.

The praise from his peers is always special for Wilson, especially when it comes from those he admires as well. "Barry Gibb loves that song and I so appreciate that," he says. "And Paul of course said that he loved it. And that it's his favorite song of all time."

But what is it about "God Only Knows" that speaks so deeply to other musicians, moving the greatest songwriters of all time to literal tears? Jardine has an idea.

"The arrangement, the melody, and the amazing flute parts. Those qualities make it what it is. And it has a timeless quality, as *The Nutcracker* has with children and people of all ages actually. When you hear the Nutcracker Suite it has that same sort of lasting beauty. That's my take," Jardine says. "I see it from a classical point of view. It stands the test of time I'd say not as a pop song, but as a classic. Arrangement wise it's brilliant. I think the session men and women have to be credited with making that possible too. We had a great group of people to work with called the Wrecking Crew. So we really benefitted from that, we all did, their participation in it. It's just a wonderful production because Brian was also known as the producer. So you had those two elements going. Not only do you have a great song, you have a great producer and a great bunch of people. That's the perfect storm of creation."

A fan of classical music, Wilson appreciates Jardine's comparison to the Nutcracker Suite. "I was influenced by Tchaikovsky; he inspired me a great deal," he says. "I did use that inspiration when writing 'God Only Knows,' among other things. I actually like that comparison."

Pet Sounds and *The Nutcracker* share something else in common—namely that they took time to develop into their iconic status. Now, of course, both "God Only Knows" and the entire *Pet Sounds* album are widely regarded as seminal works that rank near the top of every best-of list published in the last thirty years.

As Jardine remembers it, though, fans did not fully comprehend what Wilson had truly achieved at the time. Like Vincent van Gogh and other great artists, Wilson's genius was so advanced it took decades to appreciate.

"*Pet Sounds* wasn't received in any manner at the time. It was pretty much put on the back shelf almost immediately—not immediately, within the year. It wasn't a big seller, so we had a best of, or greatest hits, come out shortly after. So we didn't look at it—'God Only Knows'—as a monumental piece of music as much as a song for Carl to sing, another beautiful song," he says. "We of course loved the song, don't get me wrong. It's one of my all-time favorite songs to perform. It was a centerpiece of our set ever since, but not in terms of the greatest ever written. The whole album, it took a while, for it to take off, thirty years or so, before anyone really recognized the genius and the totality of the album itself. And of course 'God Only Knows' was one of those pinnacle pieces."

But Jardine and Wilson understood the song was built for longevity. "It's a home run. But Brian would explain it, I think, it's a long-term home run. I asked him once about the Beatles and he said the same thing about them. He said, 'The Beatles are like a big explosion, we're like a long one,'" Jardine recalls.

When told of Jardine's analogy in a separate conversation, Wilson concurred, laughing. "Yes, it is like a long-term home run. And of course it has stood the test of time. I like the baseball term."

But even if everybody didn't recognize immediately just what Wilson had accomplished, Wilson did. And it started for him with his brother Carl Wilson's vocal.

Asked if he knew at the time that he had created something that would go on to be one of the most beloved songs of all time, he has no hesitation. "Yes, I did," he says. "Carl's lead was the most memorable for me. I gave him that song to sing because he has a great voice."

Wilson recalls the song, which he cowrote with Tony Asher, who wrote the lyrics, as coming quickly and easily in the writing process. "It came from God through me. And of course Tony's lyrics," he says. "I was twenty-four when I wrote 'God Only Knows' and the rest of *Pet Sounds*. All I know is I wrote what was in my heart. And the lyrics and the music just connect with people."

CHAPTER THREE

THE DOORS

✦ "LIGHT MY FIRE" ✦

For more than five decades, the Doors' "Light My Fire" has remained an enduring classic. Continually ranked near the top of classic-rock radio countdowns, the song was named the thirty-fifth greatest song of all time by *Rolling Stone* in 2004 and the fifty-second best song of the twentieth century by the RIAA (Recording Industry Association of America).

Doors guitarist Robby Krieger, the principal songwriter of the song, says it was producer Paul Rothchild who first explained to him why the song resonated so deeply with fans.

"We were talking about this—why does everybody like it so much? [Rothchild] says, 'Three words: Light. My. Fire.' Nobody ever had thought of stringing those three words together before that time. Which is pretty amazing," Krieger says. "And that has so many meanings for people. To one guy it's lighting a joint, to another guy it's sex. One guy told me, 'Hey, I know what "Light My Fire" means.' I said, 'What?' He goes, 'It's the fire in your third eye.' He was like a meditator type of guy."

Looking back on it so many decades later, Krieger agrees with Rothchild: it is that incendiary phrase that ignites the passions of fans so deeply. "I really do think that just those three words, *light my fire*, resonate with people so much," he says.

Krieger credits legendary Doors front man Jim Morrison with inspiring the song. "When I decided to write it, I asked Jim because he was writing songs. And he said, 'We don't have enough originals. Why don't you guys try to write one?' So I said, 'All right, what should I write about?'" Krieger recalls. "And [Jim] said, 'Write about something universal that won't go out of style two years from now.' So I said, 'Okay, what's universal? Air, fire, and water. Right? What could be more universal than that?' So I picked fire, because I liked that song by the Stones, 'Play with Fire.' So that was the reason I picked fire. I think there are a lot of songs about fire. Especially after mine came out. ['I Want To Take You Higher,'] Sly and the Family Stone. So many songs about fire. But I think I was one of the first."

Krieger knew the song "Light My Fire" was special immediately. "When we played it at the Whisky [a Go Go on Sunset Boulevard], we played there every night for months and months. That's where it was obvious that 'Light My Fire' was going to be big," he recalls. "Every time we would play it live people would just go nuts. And we knew that was our best song, our most popular song. Right from the beginning."

Still, as much as fans loved the track instantly, Krieger never expected the more-than-seven-minute song, which spent three weeks at number one on the Billboard Hot 100, to become the radio smash it did.

"We never thought of it as a radio song because it was so long. So we never thought about putting it out as a single. But there was this guy, Dave Diamond, who had an FM station here in Burbank," Krieger says. "So he would play it and he would tell us all the time, 'Man, when I play "Light My Fire" all these people start calling in and requesting it again' and all this stuff. 'You guys should cut it down and get it on the AM radio.'"

To the four members of the band, though, as Krieger recalls, that wasn't initially an option. "We were totally against that because the instrumental part was my favorite part of course, and Ray [Manzarek]'s," he says. "And we just didn't want to do it. But finally, when 'Break On Through (To The Other Side)' came out, that was our first single and that didn't really top the charts. That hardly got any play. We needed another single. And we had all these great songs like 'Alabama Song (Whisky Bar),' 'The Crystal Ship'—there were a bunch of them that could have been hits in my opinion. But we knew 'Light My Fire' was the best song we had."

Understanding that the song was an obvious single, the band relented and made the edit. "So we finally gave in and said, 'Okay, let's cut it down, we'll cut the instrumental down even though it's a cool part,'" Krieger recalls. "And it worked. The biggest station at that time in LA was KHJ radio. And there was this guy, Humble Harve [Miller]. He was the big DJ. He said, 'Okay, I tell you what. If you guys play a show for me at the Cheetah for free, I'll put it on the radio.' And that was the deal. It was a payola kind of thing. And the minute he put it on there it just went crazy, the lines lit up. It went crazy from there. It got on all the AM stations and became number one."

Equally unlikely as a seven-minute-plus song becoming a radio favorite, the song crossed over to the mainstream quickly when Puerto Rican star José Feliciano recorded his version of "Light My Fire."

Though Krieger didn't initially love that version, he acknowledges the role the Feliciano version played in making "Light My Fire" a chart-topping smash. "When I first heard José's version, I didn't really like it. I said, 'Oh man that's kind of MOR [middle-of-the-road]. It's not hip enough,'" Krieger says. "Because it's kind of jazzy. But as I heard it more and more I grew to love it, especially the guitar stuff he did on it. And the thing is, once he did it everyone started doing it. Because he made it more commercial. He didn't have the long solo in there and stuff. And that really is the reason it became a standard was because of him."

Since then, over the past fifty-plus years, the song has been covered countless times, by artists as wide-ranging as Johnny Mathis, Shirley Bassey, Nancy Sinatra, Stevie Wonder, Four Tops, Al Green, Mae West, Massive Attack, and more.

There have been so many covers of the song it's impossible to keep track of them all, even for Krieger. But he has his favorites. "Did you ever hear Brian Auger's version with Julie Driscoll?" he asks. "That's one of the best of all. They had a huge hit with that in, I think, '70 over in England. It never really made it over to here but it's a great version."

Krieger believes it is because of the song's musical complexity that so many diverse musicians are drawn to it. "When I wrote the song, all the Doors songs up until then were three chords, pretty simple type stuff. And I said, 'Okay, I'm going to put every chord I know into this song, I had E-flats, A-flats, all these sharps and flats and shit,'" he says. "I think there's something like fifteen different chords in that song. And you don't notice it really because of the way it falls together. But I think that's one reason the song resonates with people, because it covers so much musical territory."

He also credits keyboardist Ray Manzarek for the song's strong and unique instrumentation.

"I think another great part of the song that people overlook is the bassline. That was Ray's, it was Ray that came up with that line. And we had a guy named Larry Knechtel who actually over-dubbed a real bass on it. And did exactly what Ray played, which was not easy on a real bass. And if you really listen close, you can hear it. There's actually both basses playing throughout the whole song. I think that's one. Another reason why it's so strong. Really that bottom end just carries it," he says. "And people don't give Ray enough credit for the way he would play the bass with his left hand and add overtone with the right hand. So it's like having two people playing at once. A lot of those songs the bass player would just play exactly what Ray played. And I think that really, in 'Light My Fire' especially, was very effective."

With the song's rich musical diversity, the band was often able to stretch it out and improvise live, leading to some very memorable versions. There is one, though, that sticks out the most for Krieger.

"Isle of Wight, that version to me is really good even though the video is not all that good because it was really dark. And Jim didn't really do much except hold on to the mic and sing," he says. "But basically I think that's one of the best versions. And that was the first time that I stuck 'My Favorite Things' into the middle of my solo. Still do today, by the way."

Another version that stands out to Krieger is from the Matrix in San Francisco in 1967, where he points out if you watch it on YouTube today you can see how the song evolved from the early versions to the version on record that stands as a classic.

"That's an interesting one because before we recorded the song, the Bach organ part intro thing was actually in the middle of the song," he says. "It wasn't an intro until we recorded it and [producer] Paul Rothchild had the idea to make that the intro because before that it was just a way to get out of the instrumental part back to the next verse."

It is in part because of YouTube and the internet that new generations of fans continue to discover the Doors and "Light My Fire" specifically. But even before the internet, that was happening to every thirteen- and fourteen-year-old throughout the world. Getting into the music of the Doors is as much a rite of passage as having a first kiss, getting to second base, learning to drive, and getting drunk for the first time.

That comes in part because of the song's continued use in popular culture in shows and movies as varied as Tom Hanks's *Cast Away*, *Altered States*, *WKRP in Cincinnati*, *More American Graffiti*, and maybe most memorably in *Family Ties*, when Michael J. Fox's Alex P. Keaton sings the song in the landmark "A, My Name Is Alex" episode.

Because it has continually been used in pop culture over the decades, and because of films like Oliver Stone's *The Doors*, the myth and mystique of the legendary LA quartet remains as strong as it was in the years following Morrison's death on July 3, 1971.

Krieger sees it in both fans and musicians. "I talk to kids a lot and I'm always amazed when they're interested in the Doors," he says. "And I always ask them, 'Did your parents play it all the time for you?' And a lot of them say, 'No, no my friend told me' or 'I looked it up online' or whatever. So I always thought, maybe it's the parents that are playing it all the time and then the kids would hear it. But I think kids discover it for themselves, 'Light My Fire,' and the Doors especially."

The same is true of musicians. "Eddie Vedder, man, when we did 'Light My Fire' at the Rock & Roll Hall of Fame induction thing, he was so into the Doors and Jim," Krieger recalls. "He took me up to his hotel room and cornered me, just grilling me about Jim. For hours. It's just amazing how these younger guys at the time were just really influenced by us."

Thanks to the enduring popularity of songs like "Light My Fire," those younger guys continue to be influenced and inspired by the Doors. And it doesn't seem like that's going to change.

CHAPTER FOUR

JEFFERSON AIRPLANE

✦ "WHITE RABBIT" ✦

*J*efferson Airplane singer Grace Slick is truly an original, the kind of artist that rock 'n' roll urban legend was invented for. In one of the most famous stories in rock, Slick once was thrown out of the White House when she got caught trying to slip acid to then president Richard Nixon.

The anecdote, from an April 24, 1970, tea party Slick was invited to by Nixon's daughter Tricia, is 100 percent true, as Slick has confirmed in past interviews. Slick didn't get to give the LSD in her pocket to Nixon because she invited Abbie Hoffman as her date and they were both on a domestic-security watch list. Would she have gotten away with it if she hadn't invited Hoffman? Who knows, but even the attempt is part of the myth of Slick.

So it is not surprising to anyone who has interviewed or spent time with Slick that she has a very unique take on the timeless success of the 1967 hit "White Rabbit," from the seminal album *Surrealistic Pillow*. One of the definitive songs of the iconic Summer of Love, "White Rabbit" became the band's second top ten song and has since been named one of the greatest songs of all time by *Rolling Stone* and the Rock & Roll Hall of Fame.

For Slick, now that she has had fifty-four years to process the song's enduring popularity—as she says in her matter-of-fact way, "I pay my electric bills and so forth with the residuals from 'White Rabbit.' And it just keeps coming in. So I'm a happy camper"—and the appeal of the song is obvious to her.

"There are two reasons for it helping to be what it is and that is because it's basically a rip-off, not literally. But Ravel's 'Boléro' is a Spanish march and *Alice in Wonderland*, everybody knows that story. So you have one genius writing the story and another genius writing the music. And I'm borrowing from both of them," she says with that trademark Slick bluntness. "And it's like a lot of people said, there's nothing new under the sun. It's all been done before or will be done again. And I didn't take it directly from Ravel's 'Boléro' and I didn't take the lyrics directly from *Alice in Wonderland*. It is paraphrased and you have to do that."

As for the second reason she believes the song has lasted for more than half a century, that answer is also vintage Grace Slick.

"The response to the song after it came out for a while was always pretty good. People liked that song. There's a reason for that," she says. "It has a buildup, the same way that sex has a buildup. You start kissing, then you start feeling around. Then you get into bed and take off your clothes and then you poke like crazy and then, oh boy! A climax. And that's the way 'White Rabbit' is. It starts off softly and comes to a climax in the end. So people are geared to like that progression."

The song actually predates her involvement with Jefferson Airplane. And she thought in the infancy of "White Rabbit" there might be something there, but it was hard to tell.

"I had played it live before recording it on *Surrealistic Pillow*. Because I was with another group called [the] Great Society. We were making fun of Lyndon Johnson's name for who he thought he was governing. The name of the group, Great Society. But I played it live with them," she recalls. "People seemed to like it. But we played for so few people. Great Society, when we were a band, we played at a dump on Broadway in San Francisco, for maybe four drunk sailors. We played several jobs a night, forty-five minutes a set and the people, the clientele were not young hippies from San Francisco. They were local drunks. Or sailors and soldiers who were off on leave for one reason or another. They didn't know what we were doing. But they seemed to like it enough."

Slick had no idea the song would become the anthem it is today. But she did know there was something about "White Rabbit" that separated it from many of the other songs in the Summer of Love.

"It's a Spanish march. We're a rock 'n' roll band and 'White Rabbit' is a Spanish march," she says. "And that's just goofy for starters. I knew it was different, but I didn't know it was going to take off the way it did."

Even in the writing and recording, Slick recalls, the song was intended to stand out from the rock 'n' roll crowd. "When I first recorded [the song] it sounded just fine in the studio. It is not a song that is hampered by the cymbals messing up the midrange. So it's a very calculated song. It's not all over the place," she says. "You can hear all the instruments. It's not difficult to separate what's going on. Sometimes, rock 'n' roll songs, there's a lot of stuff going on. And you can't separate the instruments very well."

However, Slick says that was intentionally not the case in the stripped-down—as it turns out, very stripped-down—writing of "White Rabbit." "This one was just written on a piano. That had about eight keys missing. Because when we were writing songs we didn't have any money. We lived in Larkspur, California. And it's an upright, tiny, little upright red piano that was all beat up and I got it for about fifty dollars. And I didn't mind because the notes that were missing, I didn't need those notes," she says, laughing. "So I was okay with it. And I wrote a lot of songs on that piano. I'm not a big piano player so I didn't care. I know block chords. I know how to play a C major, C minor, D major, D minor, all that. Those are block chords. So in order to write a song all you need to know is block chords. And a melody. You sing the melody, you play the block chords with your left hand, right hand. And you can write a song that way. 'White Rabbit' was written that way. And some other songs that I can't remember. But I'm so old I can't remember the names anymore."

As with all stories from Slick, the tale behind the writing of "White Rabbit" is entertaining, candid, and quite funny. And it says a lot about both her mindset and the mindset of the Summer of Love musicians in that period. Whereas today's musicians might test a song on different speakers or in different studios or live first, Slick tested "White Rabbit" in differing mindsets, let's say.

"The song took about a half an hour to write. I don't know why. Other songs take a long time or several days. What I used to like to do, but not recently because it's not PC. But what I used to do was I would write a song in one frame of mind. It could be sober, it could be marijuana. It could be a lysergic acid. It could be alcohol, it could be cocaine. Whatever I wrote it in, then I'd play it again in another frame of mind. And then play it again in another frame of mind so that it worked on all levels. Like if you're loaded on LSD it worked, if you're loaded on alcohol it worked. That happened with 'White Rabbit.' After I got through writing it, I did that process. And it works, regardless of what mood you're in."

Now that it had proof of purchase, regardless of the drug or alcohol you were on at the time, the song quickly became a favorite on radio, though others around her weren't convinced the song would become a hit.

"They played it a lot on radio. A lot. And I was all excited about that. And they said, 'Well don't get too excited. The reason they play it a lot is because it's only about a minute long. And they can get more commercials in,'" she says. "I went, 'Oh well, I don't want to hear that.' But I started noticing they played it a lot. And then the response from audiences was getting bigger and bigger. So I heard it on the radio and got the response from the audience. I appreciated that because it is a weird song."

Fittingly, since she was in LA at the time, Slick recalls the first time she heard the song on the radio was of course in the car, actually driving to the studio. "I was in LA, driving to or from RCA LA, which I think is on either Hollywood Boulevard or Sunset," she says. "But they had the best studio I've ever recorded in. Studio A at the RCA building. And it was an amazing studio. You could record either an acoustic instrument or electric and it all really worked well. And vocals. It was a big room, but the vocals worked. The first time I heard my own voice on those big Altec speakers, these giant speakers, I thought: *Oh my God, this is heaven! I'm loving this.* So I think I was driving to or from the studio for one reason or another and I heard it on radio and I thought, *Ooh, that's nice.* 'Cause I'd never really heard any of my songs on radio."

Of course once the song started getting radio airplay the audience reaction live was far different than in the dive bars where she played to four drunken sailors with the Great Society. As the Airplane took off, so to speak, they played some of the biggest events of the late '60s, including Monterey Pop in 1967 and Woodstock in 1969.

For Slick, though, there isn't one standout performance of the iconic track, even bringing a legendary anthem to an equally historic event. Rather, according to her, the song was special almost every time they performed it.

"The kids, they'd sing along with the songs they knew. And they'd sing along with that one," she recalls. "But it didn't bother it any or anything because the end is so loud that it doesn't matter. That's the one good thing about rock 'n' roll. If you're a cabaret singer and you're singing 'Stardust' by Hoagy Carmichael, and people start getting loud, you're in trouble. With rock 'n' roll, it's so loud in the first place that it doesn't matter what people are doing in the audience."

Again, she attributes the song's continual live appeal to the buildup she referred to earlier. To her, understandably, when you take that rising tension and momentum and magnify it by tens of thousands of fans screaming, "Go ask Alice, when she's ten feet tall," then reaching that climatic crescendo of "Feed your head," the electricity is palpable.

"Like I said, it takes on the progression that is natural to us. You start out slowly and you work up to something. Even planting a flower. You start off putting a little seed in the ground, you tamp it down with a trowel, then you water it a little bit, then you see the first leaves come out. Then in spring, there's this big goddamn flower that's beautiful. Everything works that way. So it's natural for us to respond to that process," she says. "'White Rabbit' starts off softly and slowly builds to that climax, 'Feed your head.' Twice, loud. So it's a natural progression. I wasn't aware of any of this stuff when I wrote it. I just wrote it because

I liked the way it worked, that way. I'm just using that progression. That thing of starting off softly and building up. You can start off loud and then go back down and then come back up. That works too. Particularly with rock 'n' roll, that to get loud sound, we're so used to loud, you can start off pretty loud and then go back down. But you have to do that, going back down, up and down. You can't just have straight all the way through. It just gets boring."

Because of that natural progression Slick mentions, the song has been covered numerous times, in styles from jazz to metal. As early as 1971 jazz greats George Benson and Herbie Hancock did the song. And in the years since, everyone from Slick's fellow Rock & Roll Hall of Famer Patti Smith, on 2007's *Twelve* album, to punk heroes the Damned have shown the song love with their interpretations.

There is one version, however, that not only stands out to Slick, but she believes exceeds the original. "I think Pink did it better than I did, vocally," she says. "I don't have that good of a voice. I have to be very careful when I either harmonize in somebody else's song or sing melody in my own songs. I have a very limited range, like Robert Plant apparently has a really big range. I don't. I have a range of about four notes and they're all right in the middle. So I can sing high loud, but I can't sing high softly. So I could never sing lullabies to my daughter when she was a baby. 'Cause I'm just too damn loud. That's just the way my voice is. So it was built for rock 'n' roll, because I definitely can be heard."

She does have some dream artists to cover the song. And her choices might surprise you. "I'd like to see Barbra Streisand do 'White Rabbit,'" she says, laughing. "Miss Broadway. Or Céline Dion. Some straight singers. I'd like to see them take a shot at it. They'd probably be pretty good. I mean they've got great voices.

And both of them have good volume. So it would be odd, but I'd like to see it. Or say even better would be an opera singer, see an opera singer do it."

It seems unlikely, but given the wide range of movies, TV shows, and video games that have featured the song, maybe it's not impossible. While the diversity of the artists who have covered the song is a testament to its universal appeal, so is the fact it has been used in both the Oscar-winning, Vietnam-era film *Platoon* and the animated TV series *Futurama*. And in between those, "White Rabbit" has appeared in *The Sopranos, American Dad, Kong: Skull Island, The Handmaid's Tale*, and on and on.

There was one instance of the song appearing in a film that really stands out to Slick. "I live in Malibu so I went to a movie theater. It was on a Tuesday or something. There was only one other person in the thing at the time. It was Sean Penn and I think Michael Douglas," she says of the 1997 David Fincher film, *The Game*. "And I had learned just a week earlier or something that when they use your song, that's about thirty thousand dollars. If they use it twice, that's sixty thousand dollars. So when they played it, I was watching that, I didn't even know that it was in the film. I don't pay attention to any of that stuff. So it came on and I went, 'Oh yeah!' And the one other person in the film turned around and looked at me because it wasn't the right response for when they were playing. And the second time they played it, I went, 'Oh yes, that's sixty thousand bucks.' And the guy just looked at me like, this woman is nuts."

As has been made apparent, Slick, now eighty-one and every bit the iconoclast she was at twenty-seven, has a pragmatic approach to the song and its success in many ways. "It was a very popular song and still gets played a lot," she says. "I have a station on my television that plays—832 is progressive rock, 883 or 833,

I forget which it is—plays nothing but classic rock. And they play it all the time. I still make money from 'White Rabbit.'"

But underneath her humor and bluntness is a tremendous artistic pride in what she created and how it still resonates so deeply with fans today.

"I like it because even though it is drawn from two other people, Ravel and Lewis Carroll, it's still very original for rock 'n' roll. At the time, you didn't have anything that was that off the wall, for rock 'n' roll. It was all standard shuffle or the beats that we have for rock 'n' roll. It wasn't a march. That's a march. And you didn't have marches for rock 'n' roll. So I'm proud of the fact that it's very unique."

CHAPTER FIVE

NEIL DIAMOND

✦ **"SWEET CAROLINE"** ✦

"Where it began, I can't begin to knowing, but then I know it's growing strong."

Great songwriters will often talk about their songs being prophetic. But when Neil Diamond wrote those opening words to "Sweet Caroline" in a Memphis hotel in 1968, he couldn't have had any clue how true those words would become more than five decades later.

The journey of "Sweet Caroline" is foretold in those opening two lines. "Where it began I can't begin to knowing," Diamond sings. As for the origin of the song, he tells me, "That song came to me—it was given to me personally by God."

Then that second line: "But then I know it's growing strong." That right there is the story of any anthem: a song that, whether it starts as a hit or not, takes years to become an anthem.

How could Diamond have any idea that when he stepped into American Sound Studio in Memphis early in 1969 to record a love song for his then wife Marcia, but using the name Caroline because of its musicality (and inspired by a photo of John F. Kennedy's daughter Caroline), that joyous, feel-good, three-minute pop song would one day go on to be one of the greatest and most unlikely sports anthems of all time?

Long before the song became synonymous with the Boston Red Sox and became a sports anthem, there were other signs Diamond had truly achieved something enduring with "Sweet Caroline."

The song became an immediate hit, reaching the top five in America, Canada, and Australia upon its 1969 release. And in an early landmark performance, Diamond performed "Sweet Caroline" in November 1969 on his only visit to *The Ed Sullivan Show.*

Seated for the whole performance, something that may never have happened again, Diamond showed an early glimpse at what a joyful celebration the song would become, earning a rousing ovation from the audience and complimentary words from the host himself, Diamond told me.

"He said some nice things to me after I did 'Sweet Caroline,'" Diamond recalls of talking to Sullivan, who also had a memorable meeting with Diamond's mother and father, who were in the audience.

"When the show was over I asked Mr. Sullivan if I could introduce my parents and he said, 'Yeah.' I went into the audience after the show was over and brought them up. She did the same thing when she met Laurence Olivier. She took a signed, autographed picture of me out of her pocket and gave it to Mr. Sullivan. She said, 'Here, keep this—he's going places.'"

For Diamond, singing "Sweet Caroline" on that hallowed stage was incredibly special. "For me to be on the same stage that

Elvis Presley was on and performed, same thing with the Beatles, I'm awed by it."

Before the song became a staple of his live sets, there was another telling indicator of the appeal of "Sweet Caroline": the response from other musicians. Diamond had enjoyed successful cover versions of his songs before, notably the Monkees on "I'm a Believer," but the list of artists who have covered "Sweet Caroline" is like a vocalist's hall of fame.

When you write a song that Elvis Presley, Frank Sinatra, Roy Orbison, Bobby Womack, Waylon Jennings, and Julio Iglesias all performed, you have clearly crafted a masterpiece. Those six iconic but disparate artists show the universality of "Sweet Caroline."

Those are rock icons in Presley and Orbison, a singer's singer and crooning legend in Sinatra, a soul hero in Womack, a member of the Country Music Hall of Fame in Jennings, and a Spanish-singing legend in Iglesias, who performed the song in Spanish.

Later, over the years, the Dave Matthews Band would cover the song, at Boston's Fenway Park, naturally. As would Me First and the Gimme Gimmes, who did a punk version; the Ventures, who went instrumental with their rendition; the cast of the TV show *Glee*; country superstar Luke Bryan; and countless more.

But those first six performers, all of whom released their versions within a decade of the initial release of "Sweet Caroline," years before it would become fashionable and cool to perform the song, prove the song's resonance with his peers.

Of all the countless covers of his songs, Diamond told me Sinatra's interpretation of "Sweet Caroline" is his favorite. "That would be Frank Sinatra's version of 'Sweet Caroline,' which he did with a big band," Diamond says. "Absolutely that would be my favorite. He did it his way, he didn't cop my record at all. I've heard that song by a lot of people and a lot of good versions of it.

But Sinatra's swinging, big band version of 'Sweet Caroline' tops them all by far."

While Diamond's early performance on *Ed Sullivan* portended the song's success with live audiences, the song would, over the years, grow into being not only one of Diamond's biggest songs live but arguably the biggest live pop anthem in the world.

"Sweet Caroline" live is the mirror of Diamond in concert, from the somewhat reserved early performance on *Ed Sullivan* to decades later, the unabashed, euphoric showman who shares everything with his audience. If you go back and listen to the 1972 *Hot August Night* version of "Sweet Caroline," you see the beginning of that performer, as he almost emphatically speaks those opening words and you hear the rising crescendo of the music the first time the iconic refrain, "Hands, touching hands, reaching out, touching me, touching you," comes in.

But then you feel the more seasoned, confident performer in later live performances of the song. Even just five years later, on the *Love at the Greek* live album, you can hear the crowd roar the instant the opening notes kick in. Then he goes into the improvisation of the song, like muttering the words, "Look out," after the lines, "But then I know it's growing strong."

That early improvisation would later become a hallmark of the song as Diamond grew into one of the all-time great live performers, who set box-office records around the globe. You hear it in full stride by the 1987 *Hot August Night II* album, in the strong, forceful opening vocals. It's also where Diamond tapped into the full potential of the song's lyrics built for the stage.

Like when he screams the line, "Who'd have believed you'd come along," eliciting a thunderous bellow from the crowd. Or he changes the line, "How can I hurt when holding you," to "How can I hurt when I'm here with you? No way," as the music swells and the audience goes wild.

The best live songs evoke a communal sense that crosses generations, like Bruce Springsteen doing "Born to Run" and Paul McCartney performing "Hey Jude." Like those songs, "Sweet Caroline" has become that song live that audiences of all ages revel in, sharing it from generation to generation.

Diamond tells us why the song is so effective live. "I add things, I take things away, I change the arrangement, I sing it a little different, the audience response is pretty much the same. They know it's a party and they join in," he says.

The song, like Diamond, has become part of family traditions. My mom, who passed in June 2018, was a huge Neil Diamond fan. And I will always remember seeing Diamond with my mom and her boyfriend and my college girlfriend at the Forum in LA. It is an indelible family memory that will include everybody, including the four of us standing and singing along to "Sweet Caroline," including the famous, "bomp, bomp, bomp."

Late, great rock icon Chris Cornell explained it so well when I spoke to him at the 2009 MusiCares tribute to Diamond. "He sort of invented iconness to me; he's one of a handful of people that was an artist I could get into that my dad liked," Cornell told me. "I remember being like six years old, seven years old, and he's made music that appeals to many different audiences and keeps going."

That cross-generational appeal is maybe never more evident than in arguably the most important performance Diamond ever did of "Sweet Caroline," in April 2013, when he surprised fans at Fenway Park to sing the song in person just five days after the horrific bombing at the Boston Marathon.

In a city reeling, Diamond showed up unannounced to lead the sold-out crowd in a rousing sing-along of the song. While it may or may not be the ultimate rendition of the song, the video that now exists on YouTube of a stadium full of fans smiling and singing along, holding "Boston Strong" signs, is inspiring and uplifting and will move you to the point of tears.

In fact, Diamond told me the performance inspired new material, which led to a portion of his 2014 *Melody Road* album. "I want the spirit of that moment, the spirit that I felt at that very moment of performing 'Sweet Caroline' for the Boston crowd, to translate into a song," he said.

By that point, "Sweet Caroline" had become a staple of Red Sox games, a tradition that dates back to 1997. According to an article on MLB.com, it was started accidentally by a woman named Amy Tobey, who was in charge of music at the stadium. She chose the song because someone she knew had just had a baby named Caroline. This being sports, she used the song only superstitiously when the Red Sox were ahead between the seventh and ninth innings.

However, as the story goes, in 2002, an executive named Dr. Charles Steinberg noticed the song's "transformative powers," as fans had at Diamond concerts for decades. And Steinberg insisted on the song being played, whether the Red Sox were winning or losing, to lift up the spirits of the crowd.[1]

While the Red Sox are the most famous team associated with "Sweet Caroline," they are far from the only ones. They weren't even the first pro sports team to play the song, as the Carolina Panthers of the NFL started using the song at home games a year earlier in 1996. It's also become part of college life at Iowa State and the University of Pittsburgh, among others.

Diamond is thankful to every and any sporting team that shares the song with their fans. "Any team that plays 'Sweet Caroline,' to me, they get it because that's the lucky song. It's not necessarily the team, it's the lucky song. And that song came to me," he says. "So I figure people pick up on that and it could become their song, their team's song. But I've heard it done by dozens of teams 'cause I think they get it the way I get it. It was given to us specially and it cruised to the team that picks it up."

There is a beautiful symmetry to the song becoming part of Major League Baseball lore, given Diamond's own boyhood love for baseball and his Brooklyn Dodgers specifically, which actually led him to music, as he recalled.

"I dreamed that the Brooklyn Dodgers would win the World Series and they did. I had to be fifteen years old before they did and I'd been rooting for the Dodgers since I was a little boy because that was always like the Boston Red Sox in Boston—it's part of the culture and the Brooklyn Dodgers were part of my life," he told me. "I remember when they left, they announced it after they won the World Series finally, and they were leaving for a far-off place, Los Angeles. I went into a real funk and I guess it prompted my parents to support the idea that maybe to cheer me up, pick me up, 'cause I was always singing, to get me some guitar lessons just to bring me out of the funk and I found something that absorbed me completely for the rest of my life."

So it is so fitting that a great part of the ascension of "Sweet Caroline" to anthem status, a fact confirmed when it was inducted into the National Recording Registry of the Library of Congress in 2019, comes from baseball. And it even made the kid who grew up loving only the Dodgers into a Red Sox fan.

"They are my second team and I love them because they showed me the love by getting on the 'Sweet Caroline' bandwagon," he told me. "They realized it was gonna be a lucky song and it was very lucky for them and lucky for me. So I was very happy to have it played there. I have a bunch of friends that are from that area in New England. So it was easy for me to root for them. And I didn't have an American League team to root for, so the Red Sox became my rooting team. And I became officially a Red Sox fan when I went there and sang for them, for the crowd, and they gave me a free hot dog. So that's like being baptized."

Then of course the last component to making "Sweet Caroline" such a significant part of American life is the frequent use in pop culture, from TV shows like *Glee* and *The Big Bang Theory* to films such as *Fever Pitch*, starring Drew Barrymore and Jimmy Fallon, about Fallon's unhealthy fandom of the Sox, and the brilliant but underrated *Beautiful Girls*, with Timothy Hutton, Uma Thurman, Matt Dillon, and more.

Both *Beautiful Girls* and *The Big Bang Theory* perfectly capture what makes "Sweet Caroline" so special and infectious. In Ted Demme's *Beautiful Girls*, Hutton sits down to play piano in a bar and as soon as he starts playing "Sweet Caroline" the entire bar sings along. And in the hit TV show *The Big Bang Theory*, there is a great scene where Amy Farrah Fowler and Howard Wolowitz are alone together for the first time and struggling mightily to find any common ground. Suddenly, a moment later they are singing along loudly and jubilantly to "Sweet Caroline."

Such is the power of the song, to bring people together. That is why it remains a force in pop culture. Just in 2020, the song was used in the new George Clooney film *The Midnight Sky* and in *Spenser Confidential*, starring Mark Wahlberg. And Diamond rerecorded the song with the London Symphony Orchestra, something he was very proud of.

"I found a formula for doing it. It was done in a completely different time change, different feel; it was done like a bolero, and that's very different," he told me.

Also in 2020, he once again put the song to use for service, as he did in Boston in 2013, revamping the lyrics a bit for a COVID pandemic public service announcement. "Hands, washing hands, don't touch me, I won't touch you," he sang on an acoustic guitar in front of a fireplace in a tweet that got over one million views in one night.

As Diamond gave new life to the classic in 2020, showing the song's timelessness and flexibility, he continues to prove that decades after he wrote the song, his words remain more prophetic as ever: "I know it's growing strong."

CHAPTER SIX

THE 5TH DIMENSION

✦ "AQUARIUS/LET THE ✦
SUNSHINE IN"

*T*he 5th Dimension's 1969 smash medley, "Aquarius/ Let the Sunshine In," spent six weeks at number one on the Billboard Hot 100, eventually being named the seventy-third biggest single of all time, and sixty-sixth greatest song of all time by the industry staple, *Billboard*. It won two Grammys, Best Contemporary Vocal Performance by a Group and the prestigious Album of the Year. And the American Film Institute named the song number thirty-three on its "100 Years . . . 100 Songs" list.

In short, the 5th Dimension marriage of "Aquarius" and "Let the Sunshine In," from the musical *Hair*, is a certified classic. However, as the 5th Dimension's Marilyn McCoo and Billy Davis

Jr. tell the story, their contribution to musical history would not have happened without a New York City cab.

"Billy had lost his wallet in a taxicab in New York City and the next guy who got into the cab was one of the producers of *Hair*. And he found Billy's union card in the wallet and called and found out that the group was performing in New York City," Mc-Coo says.

"At the Royal Bar at a hotel," Davis interjects.

"He was kind enough to call Billy and say, 'I've got your wallet.' And so Billy said, 'Well I'll come and get it.' So Billy went over and got it and then he was so thankful that he invited the man to come and see the 5th Dimension perform," McCoo recalls. "He came with his wife and saw the group. And then he turned around and invited all of us to come and see *Hair*. And we all wanted to go see *Hair* because it was such a big hit. And he was able to get us tickets but we were scattered throughout the audience."

So the five members, seated all over the theater, took in the performance and once there the magic happened instantaneously when they heard the song. "When we first heard it being performed it was Ronnie Dyson at the production of *Hair*. It was like, we have to do that song. We knew that this is a 5th Dimension song. So we called our producer right away," Davis recalls.

As McCoo remembers that night, all five members, watching the show separately, had the same feeling of inevitably that they had just seen their musical future. "So after Ronnie Dyson sang 'Aquarius,' and the intermission was shortly after that, we all met together in the lobby and said, 'Oh my God, we've got to record that song! It's a hit, it's a 5th Dimension song!'" McCoo says.

With their enthusiasm and conviction that they had heard a 5th Dimension hit, they reached out to their producer, as McCoo recalls. "We called our producer, Bones Howe, and said, 'We've got to do this song. This is going to be a 5th Dimension hit.' And he said, 'Well, I don't know.' Because what we didn't know was that there were then two or three versions that had already come out, and nothing had happened with them," she says. "But then Bones had come up with the idea of taking the song 'The Flesh Failures/Let the Sunshine In,' and putting it together with 'Aquarius.' So we went into the studio with that, and Bob Alcivar, who was our wonderful vocal arranger, came up with some beautiful ideas for harmonies and everything like he always did. And that was how that song came together."

McCoo remembers the Vegas recording session, including Davis's legendary improvisations, vividly. "We were recording in Las Vegas at the Riviera Hotel. And we were working two shows a night, seven nights a week. And then going into the studio and recording in the afternoon. But of course, we were very young," she says, laughing. "So we had recorded 'Aquarius' and we were singing the tag, which was 'Let the Sunshine In,' and Bones had come up with that. He just felt that the combination was going to work. And we sung 'Let the Sunshine In' over and over again. So after that was done, Bones said to Billy, 'Okay, Billy, now you go on in there and take it to church.' And Billy started singing all his ad libs over the song and I mean, we were jumping up and down in the studio. We were so excited about it. And then one of Billy's famous ad libs was, 'I want you to sing along with the 5th Dimension.'"

At that moment, she says as she laughs, the band got swept up in Davis's fervor and became fans of the song as much as musicians working on the track. "When we heard that we all just jumped up and down and said, 'Oh my God, that's brilliant, that's great, that's so much fun.' And I'd say then that we just felt like, 'Oh this has got to be a hit.'"

"Yeah, you never know if it's going to be a hit but we had good feelings about that one," Davis adds.

Once it did become a hit it became an instant fan favorite live and, as they both recall, the centerpiece of their Vegas show, a time Davis remembers fondly. "We didn't do the song onstage before we recorded it. We always recorded and then did the song onstage. And I remember doing 'Aquarius/Let the Sunshine In' onstage and it was a hit. Don't forget, it had been a hit. And everyone was waiting to hear it. It was just beautiful," he says. "Because during that time when we were working in Vegas, we had strings, we had harps, we had horns, we had a whole orchestra behind us. So when we do the song, it sounded just like the record. Onstage live. I'll never forget those times. I've always wanted to go back to that, but we can't go back. But those were beautiful times to hear your stuff sound just like the record, live. Yes, and the excitement that goes on, the energy in the room. Amazing, amazing."

The song, which became the set closer right away, was such a massive fan favorite live that sometimes fans, who knew the song was coming, took the whole "I want you to sing along with the 5th Dimension" part a little too literally.

"Usually we would end the show with that song. And people would start coming down the aisles and start coming up on the stage. And it became a happening. It was a real happening. There were occasional times when the audience would just take over the stage. There was one time when were onstage and everybody had left the stage. The group had left the stage because that was the only way we were going to get out of there," she recalls. "And now we're standing in the wings and I'm hearing Billy's voice still singing. And I'm saying, 'Oh my God, Billy's out there.' And then I'm worried that people are going to realize that Billy's out there, and they're going to start taking a chunk of his hair, a piece of his vest. And I said, 'We've got to go back out there and get him while he's still in one piece.'"

In the last five decades plus, the song has had a huge impact on popular culture. It's been featured in such box-office smashes as *The Forty-Year-Old Virgin* and *Forrest Gump* and is a regular on TV as well, having been used in *The Simpsons*, *Family Guy*, Carl Sagan's *Cosmos*, and *American Horror Story: Murder House*, among many other shows. The song has even become a popular soccer chant in Argentina.

Musically it's been covered by way too many artists to list them all, but among the renowned musicians who have put their spin on the medley crafted and made famous by the 5th Dimension are Diana Ross, Engelbert Humperdinck, Andy Williams with the Osmonds, Hans Zimmer, Mos Def, the Spencer Davis Group, Donna Summer (when she was cast in the 1968 German version of *Hair*), and more. It's been done in jazz styles, instrumentally by the Ventures, and even by legendary actress Raquel Welch on her 1970 TV special, *Raquel!* Maybe the most famous version is the crowd at Woodstock singing the song, which ended up on the double album *Woodstock Two*.

"We're always delighted whenever we watch *Forrest Gump* when they play 'Aquarius.' We love that moment," McCoo says.

Though, Davis adds, they're often not even aware when the song is being used. "A lot of times they will be in shows or these things that you're talking about, a lot of times we didn't know they were even in there," he says. "Sometimes our friends would call us and say, 'Hey, did you know that we heard your song in *The Forty-Year-Old Virgin*?' 'What?' Those things happen because there's so much going on out there you just can't keep up with everything. But yes, we're very glad that our stuff is in there."

For all of the iconic names that have tried their hand at the song, there is one moment that stands out for Davis, that one moment where he knew the version he and his bandmates had done would forever be etched in pop culture lore.

"One of the things when I knew that it had become an anthem was when we did 'Let the Sunshine In' and 'Aquarius,' and it got to be so big that when they put it back up on Broadway, they had to do it the way we had recorded it," he says, pointing out that the Flesh Failures version was nothing like the 5th Dimension interpretation. "They did the 5th Dimension version. And that's when I said, 'Wow, that song has really hit its height.'"

McCoo concurs that hearing their rendition on Broadway was an unexpected and joyful surprise. "The one that Billy just referred to really stood out for me. The fact that when they brought *Hair* back, after all those years and they started to perform 'Aquarius' and 'Let the Sunshine In' as the 5th Dimension version surprised me because I thought that we were going to hear the original version again," she says. "And they put the two songs together. That was the one thing that stood out for me because I said, 'Oh my gosh, what an impact our version had on that song and on the show.' Because they took it and our version became their version."

Over the years the 5th Dimension became a favorite of kids from a very unlikely recording. "We had the opportunity to record the Declaration of Independence [as the 'The Declaration']. And we didn't know that that song would one day be such a tool for teaching kids in school," Davis says. "And a lot of teachers through the years have told us that song helped them to teach kids the Declaration of Independence though music. How they would learn the words through it and remember them. And we didn't know it, we were just singing it during that time, that was our protest song during that time during those years. But the teachers took it and used it in school as a teaching tool. And they told us that years ago and I'd say, 'Oh my God, that was a good thing because it taught so many kids the Declaration of Independence.'"

Still, thanks to "Aquarius/Let the Sunshine In" being used in movies and TV shows, it is and always will be the song the group is best known for, including among kids. And they see the results of that every time they play live.

"Yes, yes, we have found that," Davis says. "When we do 'Aquarius' today, and 'Let the Sunshine In,' even the young kids jump up and down. And it's amazing to see it. It blows your mind that this is still happening, that the song would do that."

As much as she enjoys that, for McCoo it's seeing the response from those who have lived with the song for fifty years that is the most meaningful to her. "But you know one thing that I'm always moved over, we see people, gray hair, people our age, older, a little younger, but our—in our age group they still storm the stage," she says, laughing.

"Like they go back inside! It's like, 'What are these old folks who are running down the stage?!" Davis adds. "They don't come up onstage but they do run down to the front of the stage."

For McCoo it's special to see them appreciating their memories and what the song means to them. "They come all the way down to the front of the stage. They dance. They want you to put the mics in their mouths so they can sing with you," she says. "It's such a beautiful thing to see. Because they're reliving their youth. It's so wonderful to know that we help to make those moments special in people's lives. It really is beautiful."

CHAPTER SEVEN

CROSBY, STILLS, NASH & YOUNG

✦ "OUR HOUSE" ✦

ometimes greatness practically writes itself. One hour. That's how long it took Graham Nash to sit at a piano in the Laurel Canyon home he shared at the time with Joni Mitchell and pen "Our House" about their life together.

On a 1969 Saturday morning, after having breakfast at Art's Delicatessen on Ventura Boulevard, the live-in lovers passed an antique store on the way back to the car and Nash convinced Mitchell to buy a vase. When they got back to their home in Laurel Canyon, Nash said, "Why don't you put some flowers in the vase?" Then he lit a fire and an hour later the definitive anthem of domestic bliss was born.

It's easy to picture the innocence and sweetness of Nash sitting down on that rainy Saturday afternoon to play "Our House" for Mitchell that first time. Young and in love, unfettered by a history and believing that the message of the song and their domestic bliss would indeed be forever as he serenaded her with the tune.

Of course that didn't happen. The two did not end up together and as former lovers didn't always have the simplest relationship. That is why, for Nash, the most memorable performance of the song for Mitchell is not the first time he played it for her. Rather, the most meaningful, for him, is the last time he played it for her, a full five decades after he wrote "Our House."

In November 2018, Nash had the honor of serenading Mitchell, along with an audience that included Elton John, Brandi Carlile, Cameron Crowe, and countless more luminaries at a concert celebrating Mitchell's seventy-fifth birthday at the Dorothy Chandler Pavilion in Los Angeles.

"When I was asked to perform at Joni's seventy-fifth birthday show in Los Angeles, everyone was doing a Joni song," he explains. "But I've never done a Joni song. So I thought it was okay for me to do that. It wasn't that I was singing one of my songs about something else. It was the song that I'd written for her. And to look up in the last chorus and see Joni singing 'Our House' to me fifty years later was a pretty interesting emotion. For me to look around and see all the people on the show, singing the song to Joni, who was singing it back to us was incredible."

That iconic performance not only brought the history of the song, and their relationship, full circle—it brought the song's classic improvisational feel full circle as well.

As Nash explains, the famous la-las came about spontaneously in the studio, courtesy of Stephen Stills.

"It really was a suggestion of Stephen Stills," Nash recalls. "I think when we got to 'Our House,' I think it was Stephen who told me, 'I've done a lot of solos, on the first record; on this record, let's do something different for a solo.' And I said, 'We should just la-la-la the way through it.' He goes, 'Yeah.' We worked out the harmonies and it worked out perfectly. It just shows you that genius of Stephen Stills."

Well that night, fifty years later, as Nash sat at a piano and looked out at Mitchell a few rows away from the stage, fellow musicians Emmylou Harris and Rufus Wainwright played the parts of Stills and David Crosby, lending their vocals for the la-las, which Nash says was also improvised.

"It was a pretty loose show. There were a lot of great musicians and a lot of great music that was going to be played but not a lot of time to rehearse. It was very spontaneous," he says.

The simple beauty of the song, which is warm and inviting, is so much of the magic of "Our House." Though Nash is singing about his and Mitchell's house in Laurel Canyon, it is everybody's home.

Nash knew when he wrote the song he had captured something special. "Being a single-oriented, pop rock 'n' roll musician all my life, when I hear a piece of music, I can immediately transform it to the radio and see what it sounds like on the radio or on the TV, coming out of speakers or a small transistor at the beach," he says. "You can sense that what I'd just produced was going to be a popular song. I didn't know that it would be so popular, and I certainly didn't know that it was going to be listened to fifty years later."

That Nash had no idea how timeless the song would go on to become is not surprising. Talk to any musician and they will tell you that being in the midst of making a record or a successful tour is like being in the eye of a hurricane. Everything comes flying at you with rapid speed and you are ducking, moving, running, just trying to get to the next safe space.

So it often takes years for an artist to be able to appreciate or understand how deeply a song can resonate with listeners. For Nash that moment came when he returned to his native UK in 1974, as the triumphant hero coming home.

"When CSNY was playing the last show of our stadium tour in 1974, the last show was at the Wembley Stadium outside London. Anywhere from eighty to one hundred thousand people," he recalls. "It was the first time we had been to England in several years. I knew that when I sat down to play 'Our House' they would recognize it. But their response at the end was insane for me. It was a truly magnificent response. I mean, when one hundred thousand people are genuinely applauding what you just did, as a musician it's an incredible feeling. I remember that night very, very well."

It was five years after writing the song for Mitchell that Nash could see how special the song was on its way to becoming. Now, fifty years later, Nash can step back and understand why the song has become the timeless classic it is today.

"Everybody I know has a house. So 'Our House' is immediately recognizable to a majority of people. I think that the warmth of the record and what the record was about, my relationship with Joni, I think people could really relate to it on a very personal level," he says.

That universal appeal has made "Our House" a staple work in popular culture, from *The Simpsons* and *How I Met Your Mother* to *Cheers* and the 1994 film *My Girl 2*. On *Cheers*, Frasier Crane and his wife, Lilith (played by actors Kelsey Grammer and Bebe Neuwirth), sang the song on the occasion of moving into their new apartment.

Most recently, an episode of the Emmy-winning *This Is Us* built an entire episode around the song and Rebecca Pearson's (Mandy Moore) love of Joni Mitchell. In parallel stories Rebecca visits Mitchell's home in Los Angeles with her husband Jack Pearson (Milo Ventimiglia) and son Kevin (Justin Hartley) and talks about the history of the song "Our House."

To Nash, there is no greater honor than other artists, whether it is film and TV or musicians like Helen Reddy, Phantom Planet, and Sheena Easton, bringing their own visions and interpretations of the song to life.

"I enjoy it when people cover my songs. It means they must love it," he says. "And therefore, it means that I must have been successful in writing something that they can appreciate and love."

It is an incredible journey the song has taken from when Nash first recorded the song at Wally Heider's Studio 3 in Los Angeles. "I knew that once we finished that record that that was going to be a hit. And it was the same thing with 'Teach Your Children,'" he says, "Once again, Stephen didn't want to play a solo because he'd played many solos. And David [Crosby] said, 'Hey, you know, [Jerry] Garcia is in the next studio and he's been playing pedal steel for a couple of weeks. What do you think?' I said, 'We'll play Jerry the song and if he likes it and wants to play, fantastic.' And Jerry had his pedal steel in the other studio, we were in Wally Heider's Studio C in San Francisco. The [Grateful] Dead were in one studio, we were in one studio, and Jefferson Airplane were in another studio. So Jerry brought his pedal steel into our studio, put it on, one take. Fantastic!"

Today, when Nash performs the song he transports himself back to being at the piano in that Laurel Canyon home on a rainy Saturday afternoon in 1969. "When I play 'Our House' lately, I try and sing it with the same emotion and the same passion as when I wrote it," he says. "Because I believe that I owe it to my fans to give them the sonic experience that they cling onto in their memories."

He owes it to those fans because those fans have shared with him and told him the stories of how the song has become part of their lives and their homes. "Fans have told me, in very warm sentences, exactly what that song means to them. And it makes me realize that in that particular song, I nailed down a very common, beautiful feeling of warmth and having a home and having a safe place to be," he says. "And having a safe place to grow up and having a safe place to have a relationship with a woman. I think I really nailed it."

That people all over the globe, from families in Idaho to Istanbul, emulate Frasier and Lilith from *Cheers* and Rebecca and Jack from *This Is Us* and sing the song when they move into a new home, that it has become part of family lore and a cultural touchstone prove that Nash did nail it. For him, as the writer of this simple ditty written in an hour, as a love song to the woman he was living with at the time, there is no greater compliment to the song.

"I hope that they will understand the love that the song was written with," he says of the millions who sing the song today and will for decades, if not centuries, to come. "The passion that I had for the woman that I was living with, Joni. And I think because everyone is going to get married and move into their house, they're obviously going to love it and I love that because it extends the life of the song. Which is what I intended in the first place. I wanted as many people to hear it as possible. I don't mind if one hundred thousand people are singing my song back to me. I don't mind that. I think that's an incredible investment in emotion the crowd has that they are paying me back for the song that I wrote for Joni."

CHAPTER EIGHT

THE JACKSON 5

✦ "ABC" ✦

𝒮ometimes the symbolism is so obvious it just writes itself. In April 1970, the Beatles had their second-to-last number one song with the title track to the *Let It Be* album. The song spent two weeks at number one, the weeks of April 11 and 18, before being displaced by the Jackson 5's "ABC."

Let It Be was the Beatles' final studio album to be released after a half decade of dominating the music world in a way that was never seen before and that will never be matched.

"ABC," meanwhile, was the second of four number one songs that year from Gary, Indiana's Jackson 5: brothers Michael, Tito, Jermaine, Jackie, and Marlon.

Little more than a decade later, with 1982's *Thriller*, which topped the charts for most of 1983, Michael Jackson would go on to become the biggest artist in the world and perhaps the closest act to ever rival the success and dominance of the Beatles (ironically, the Jackson 5 also dethroned the Beatles four months later with the brothers' "The Love You Save" knocking "The Long and Winding Road" out of the top spot).

So the symbolism of the young upstart brothers on their second album, 1970's *ABC*, scoring four number one songs in the year of the Beatles' demise and ascending to the top of the pop world seems obvious. As the Beatles called it quits, there was a spot for a new ruler of the pop world and the Jackson 5 were definitely contenders for that throne.

More than five decades later, Tito Jackson says the brothers were aware of the Beatles but not old enough to understand the significance of what they had accomplished or what it meant to the pop culture landscape.

"We were young, we were kids. We were happy just that we had another hit record that went number one," he says. "I don't think we looked at it as a competition or anything of that nature. We were too young to understand that type of thing. But to recognize it today, that is a big thing, a success in our career. But somebody would eventually have done it, whether it was the Jacksons or whatever. The [Beatles] wouldn't have been number one the rest of the musical life," he adds.

Since they were just kids when they started, the Jackson 5 didn't quite appreciate the company they were keeping. Looking back on the number one songs of 1970, the list is beyond iconic. In a year they had four chart-toppers, other number ones besides the two Beatles singles included Simon & Garfunkel's "Bridge Over Troubled Water," Edwin Starr's "War," Diana Ross's "Ain't No Mountain High Enough," George Harrison's "My Sweet Lord," Neil Diamond's "Cracklin' Rosie," and songs from Sly and the Family Stone, Bread, Carpenters, and more. You could do a whole anthems book just on the number one songs of that year.

But, as Tito recalls, they weren't thinking about being number one with some of the greatest acts of all time, or competition. They were too young, he says, to be worried about that.

"We understood that we had turned professional as kids. I may have been sixteen. Because I know when 'I Want You Back' came out I was fifteen. And 'ABC' came out within that same year, I believe," he says. "But anyhow, being young, we knew the Beatles were very successful number one rock 'n' roll and everyone saw them come over to America. Especially those of us in show business, we like music, whatever. And we know that up on *The Ed Sullivan Show* and the girls going crazy over them. We knew of their success but we didn't understand the success; that's what I'm trying to say. That significance. Therefore we were just young kids doing our music and that's the way it was for us."

As stated, "ABC" was the quintet's second consecutive number one, coming just three months after "I Want You Back" led them to the pinnacle of the Billboard Hot 100 for the first time. And Tito Jackson admits he wasn't sure "ABC" was the right follow-up to "I Want You Back."

"I knew something was there but I didn't think what was there was as powerful as the previous song, which was 'I Want You Back.' So therefore, I did have my doubts about whether or not it would outsell 'I Want You Back' or continue to build the career," he says. "But once it was released—and also we made a splash on some major television shows such as *Ed Sullivan* and others—at that time it just really took off and the public loved it and it was a major hit for us, a number one song."

His reservations about the song back then are exactly what have made it such a timeless classic. He felt that it might be a bit simplistic. Though now most agree it is that youthful joy and innocence that make it one of the happiest songs of all time.

"I thought the song was a little young, saying 'ABC one two three.' But then when you hear it, it's really cleverly done. The melodies and the rhythms of it as well. That made me enjoy the song," he says. "But I thought it was a little young, me being a little older than Michael. Because I believe Michael was only something like, maybe ten years old when he sang that song. I remember putting him up, not me personally . . . but they used to set up a Coca-Cola wooden box that he was standing on to reach the microphone. Be equal to the brothers on certain parts, singing on the sessions. So it was a fun time in our career. I believe that it was one of the best moments that we had. But it's a great thing, it's a great thing."

In the annals of music, the stories of brothers who fight could've and did fill up whole seasons of melodramas like VH1's *Behind the Music*. There were the Kinks' Ray and Dave Davies, Oasis' Liam and Noel Gallagher, the Black Crowes' Chris and Rich Robinson, the Everly Brothers' Phil and Don Everly, and Creedence Clearwater Revival's John and Tom Fogerty. And those are just five—there are plenty more.

Perhaps because of their age and their view of music more as fun than a career at that point, Tito reflects on that time with his brothers, all five of them touring the world together, as some of the happiest times of his life.

"That makes it very special. And then, I and my brothers get along a lot better than the tabloids say. We're brothers, we're of course gonna have our bickers. [But] me and my brothers get along great. We do have our moments of disagreements but it's not crazy. We're not physical or anything like that," he says. "There's no physical thing happening there. And it's a great thing because performing with your brothers is different. Because it's a special love there for what you're doing as a family or as brothers. And I just enjoy working with my brothers more than anything."

When you are in the midst of the kind of worldwide success the Jackson 5 were achieving in 1970, everything becomes a blur. You are moving from gig to gig, taping all the biggest TV shows in the world, meeting fans around the country. There is no time to process all that is happening, let alone take the time to sit and appreciate the magnitude of claiming the mantle of one of the biggest musical acts in the world.

It's only now, more than five decades later, that Tito can sit back and understand how truly special that time was, performing with his brothers on the biggest stages in the world. And the absolutely surreal experiences he got to share with his brothers.

"I have people come in saying 'I'll Be There' or this song or that song was our wedding song. 'We danced to that song.' Or 'My first child was conceived on that,' whatever," he says. "Looking back, performing for the Queen of England and reading about it in school. And actually meeting her, stuff like that. And all that was great but when you look at how big it really, really was, it was big stuff as a kid, and I can appreciate my career at this time. But you're absolutely right: you do not realize what you're doing, when you're doing it." When he saw his life story turned into an Emmy-winning miniseries, *The Jacksons: An American Dream*, in 1992, decades before the music biopic craze of recent years, that is when he understood how special what they had accomplished was.

"It's just something that comes with age and looking back at your career. And there was a Jackson story, *American Dream*, that came on television, and it shows some of the accomplishments that you've done in the past. You start to realize you're making history, musical history I should say," he says. "And when they want to display you in museums and things of that nature. We have a full dedication of a Hard Rock Casino in west Indiana—Gary, Indiana—that we opened just a few weeks ago. It was a great journey, man. It was a time in my life, for sure, that I'll always put in the forefront, as a young man having such success."

Sure, here were five kids from Gary, Indiana, who loved music and had watched the greats on *Ed Sullivan* and *American Bandstand*, and now they were on those iconic stages.

To him the most memorable performance was their December 1969 appearance on *The Ed Sullivan Show*, a performance that is now seen as iconic in pop culture history.

"*The Ed Sullivan Show* was very nice. And Dick Clark as well. Because we had all grown up watching *American Bandstand*," he recalls. "Therefore that was a good time, meeting Dick Clark. And performing on his *American Bandstand*. But of course, *The Ed Sullivan Show* was the highlight because everyone would watch that on a Sunday evening. And that show really, I think, put eyes on the Jackson 5 and the music that we were doing at that time. So I look at that as our launching television appearance."

If *Ed Sullivan* was the launching pad, they made it to the television equivalent of the moon and back in the early seventies, circling all the biggest stars in the TV universe.

"Yeah, we did *Soul Train*, we did a lot of shows at the time, Flip Wilson, Bob Hope—you name them, we did it," he says. "We did a lot of television promotion, because that's what I look at as the internet today. That was the way of promoting and marketing your record."

With their successful television appearances taking them to the mountaintop of the pop music world, the next step was touring. As Tito recalls it that was often interesting because the band's success and the youthful fervor of the fans combined to send the crowds into a frenzy, often very early in the set.

"I remember a lot of times that we would perform, we wouldn't get past or get finished with the second song because the fans would rush the stage," he says. "And we'd have to run for our lives. So that was an exciting time in our career. When your fans can actually love you and hurt you at the same time."

As such, they often didn't even to get to "ABC" in the set. So it's difficult for him to pinpoint the most iconic early performances of the song. But coming back to *The Ed Sullivan Show* in May 1970 for an encore appearance and doing "ABC" there was very special for him.

"I just know when we did it on *The Ed Sullivan Show* it was very exciting, it just felt good," he says. "And we were still building at that time. We were building our catalog of music and all those things. Every time you get something that's very interesting to the public and they're digging it, it's a great feeling. To know that they like your craft, you're doing a great job, and you deserve to be amongst the bigger musicians, that just comes with the territory."

Now with both artists and audiences older, calmer, more dignified, and less frenzied, the remaining brothers are able to do the song live and see how it has become a massive live favorite.

"It's one of our bigger songs. We do 'ABC' in a medley now onstage. Because there's so many songs to be done. It's one of the bigger responses. We do 'I Want You Back,' 'The Love You Save,' 'I'll Be There.' We do our first four number one records that we had in a row," he says. "And so 'ABC' gets a very nice response, a big response at that time. Everyone sings along in the chorus. Everyone is aware of the song and just loves the song."

Part of that audience recognition comes from the song's frequent use in popular culture since its release. As a song that generates immediate audience familiarity and feelings of happiness, "ABC" has become one of the most utilized songs in media.

It's been a part of TV shows (*Dancing with the Stars, Happy Endings, Vinyl, The Block, Gilmore Girls, Chicago Hope, Lizzie McGuire, Glee, The Wonder Years*), movies (*Clerks II, College Road Trip, The Italian Job, Daddy Day Care, Dick*, and others), video games, commercials, and more.

It's always been a source of pride and joy for Tito to see how the song has become a part of pop culture. "I have noticed that it's used in a lot of cartoon things, things of that nature as well," he says. "It is good feelings, it makes you feel good. People love the song, they love the music. They love what you did. As well as having the song, you have to deliver it. And it makes you feel that you did a good job."

For all the success and accolades, including "ABC" being inducted into the Grammy Hall of Fame in 2017, nothing can top the personal touch, being able to interact with fans of the song. That is where he gets to appreciate the song's impact the most.

"I was sitting outside my home in Calabasas. And this young lady was walking home from school," he recalls. "And she says, 'Hello, Mr. Jackson, you know what my favorite song is?' I say, 'What is your favorite song?' She says, '"ABC," I just love that song. I listen to it every day.' And this is a little girl. I think she must have been in maybe the sixth grade. It's just covered all the time; it's one of those songs that will be here for generations to come in the future."

CHAPTER NINE

CARLY SIMON

✦ "ANTICIPATION" ✦

*F*ive decades after "You're So Vain" became a signature hit in the seventies, Carly Simon is still keeping some of the mystery of the song, revealing only that the second verse is about actor Warren Beatty (verses one and three remain under lock and key).

However, she has no such trouble talking about the inspiration for her Grammy-nominated 1971 smash, "Anticipation." She has previously admitted the song was written while waiting for a dinner date with fellow singer-songwriter Cat Stevens. But there is a lot more to the story, including the fact that if it weren't for Stevens, she might never have started performing live.

"I wrote it when I had a date with Cat Stevens. And I was waiting for him to come over to my apartment, I was cooking him dinner. We had just played at the Troubadour together. I had opened for him and that was the only reason I started performing," she recalls. "That's the only reason that I started performing was that I was asked to open for Cat Stevens. And he was my favorite artist at the time. He still is probably. I couldn't turn that down, so I ended up opening for Cat Stevens at the Troubadour. April 6, 1971. And so then when we got to New York, I was going to open for him at Carnegie Hall but there were a couple of days before we were going to do that show. And so I invited him over to my house for dinner."

As Simon remembers it, he was not that late—fifteen, twenty minutes at most—but that was all she needed to write the song.

"I used to call him Steve, not Cat Stevens. His name is Steve Demetre Georgiou. And so in the time that I was waiting for the doorbell to ring—I lived in an apartment in Murray Hill—it was a six floor, two apartments on each floor. And I'd gotten dressed and he wasn't there yet and I was nervous," she remembers. "And I sat down on the bed with my guitar. I just started trying to imitate him. And I got that thing that he gets in his voice where he gets very tense for a minute. 'I know many fine-feathered friends.' Do you know that song, 'Hard Headed Woman'? So I was waiting for him and sitting down trying to imitate his style. While I had the guitar, just to get out of some of my nervousness. Sometimes I just play the guitar loud if I'm nervous. Some people hit pillows, I play the guitar, exaggerate the emphasis of my playing the strings. So I was doing that and going, 'Anticipation,' because I was waiting for him to show up. I was anticipating his arrival. So I just started the song and I wrote the whole song, words and music, before he got there that night. So in about fifteen minutes I wrote the whole song. Three verses and the choruses and the outro. That's only one of three times that that's ever happened to me. That I just sat down and wrote the whole song in just one stretch. It was only about twenty minutes that he was late."

Before she carries on with the story behind the song, to paint the proper picture, I have to ask what Carly Simon cooks for a dinner date with Cat Stevens. "I was making chicken with cherries in a béarnaise sauce," she says. "I was into Dione Lucas a lot in those days and her cookbook and was taking things out. And that was a great recipe."

As she mentioned, the date was in advance of opening for Stevens at Carnegie Hall. So remarkably the first ever live performance of "Anticipation" came at one of the most hallowed venues in the world. And she knew from that performance the song was going to be a hit.

"I sang it at the Carnegie Hall concert, which was just a few days after the dinner with Cat Stevens. And it was the song that got the most applause. People didn't know my material that much because I had appeared at the Troubadour for a week and the next thing was Carnegie Hall. So people didn't know the song, yet it still got such a reaction," she says.

The overwhelming positive response to the song extended to her label as well, creating a lot of pressure, as she recalls. "At that concert, Paul Samwell-Smith [an English musician and producer who cofounded the Yardbirds] had been flown over by Jac Holzman to see me because Jac wanted Paul to produce my next album, which was *Anticipation*," she says. "It was called *Anticipation* then. Had the song 'Anticipation' on it and guess why it was called *Anticipation*? Because of the song. So there was a lot of pressure put on that song because everybody thought it was a hit. Everybody thought there was something really special about it."

She vividly remembers that Carnegie Hall show, not surprising given the monumental circumstances of playing one of her first shows, debuting a new song, and opening for her favorite artist at such an iconic venue. Looking back on it she can understand why the response to that song was so powerful.

"My delivery was very strong at Carnegie Hall. Because I hadn't sung it at the Troubadour because I hadn't written it yet. So it was only a couple days before the Carnegie Hall concert. And so it was so new to me," she says. "So it was a combination of really scared: Was I going to remember it? Was I going to remember all the chords and all the words and everything? And also just knowing that it was good, that it was catchy and people really were drawn to it."

All of the excitement that night is interwoven, for her, with the heady company she was keeping as she began her career. "So after the show that night, Paul Samwell-Smith came back to the greenroom to meet me. And it was thrilling to meet him—because also I wanted Peter Asher [a member of Peter and Gordon before becoming a big music industry manager] to produce my next album after the first one. Because I was kind of the hot girl in town. That was really fun," she says, laughing. "And everybody wanted to work with me, everybody wanted to know me. It was a very exciting time. And during that time I met James [Taylor], too, doubly exciting. And so Paul came back to meet me and Paul had produced Cat Stevens albums."

Although the song was an instantaneous hit both live and with her label, she recalls the recording process as being difficult because, as she said, with the feeling the song was going to be successful there was an expectation for the recorded version to match the hype of the Carnegie Hall debut, as well as subsequent performances she did of the song in Philadelphia and Boston. All told, she estimates it was performed five times before the recording.

"It had a lot of pressure on it when we got into the recording studio. Because we knew it was going to be a hit, there was that energy around it," she says. "So we couldn't get the version of it on record, we couldn't get the excitement on the record that we had in the live performance. And we kept on cutting it, almost every recording session we cut it anew. We were trying to get that flame. But there was too much pressure on it. At first it was over-produced. We had strings or things that weren't on the live performance. And then eventually we just cut back to the way it was performed live which was me on twelve string, Jimmy Ryan on six string—no, Jimmy was playing bass. I was the only one on guitar. And then Paul Glanz was playing the piano part and Andy Newmark was playing the drums. And I think Cat Stevens sang on the chorus. I know he sang on a bunch of tunes on that album. He sang backgrounds. That's pretty impressive, isn't it?"

For all the strain and difficulty recording the song, they finally did get it right according to her label head at Elektra Records, music industry legend Jac Holzman.

"We recorded it in London at Morgan Studios. And then Paul and I came back to America to play it for Jac Holzman. Because in those days, you didn't send things by MP3s," she says, laughing. "So I remember going back and playing it for him the first time. There was no way of sending it except by a disc. By a big, heavy disc and so we didn't want Jac to hear it like that so we went back in person and played it for him. And he loved it, he was absolutely crazy about it. So that was a success but it took us the whole recording time of that album to get that one track right."

Funnily enough, though Simon remembers every last detail about the writing and the recording, from what she made Stevens for dinner to playing the song for Holzman, she admits the timeline once the song was done, starting with the artwork, is a bit of a blur.

"I had taken the album cover photo while we were in London, there in Regent's Park in front of that gate. My brother came over and shot that picture. And then we took the artwork back to New York. So we finished recording in October, I would say," she recalls.

Though she remembers there being a gap between the album being completed and the release, the single and album both came out in November 1971, right after the record was done. She says that makes sense.

"So maybe they came out simultaneously. There was a big crush to finish the artwork. I guess as soon as Jac Holzman heard it he wanted to put it out. There was still the feeling that maybe Jac wasn't going to like all the songs that I'd written for it. Because Jac still thought I was more of a singer than a writer," she says. "On the first album, I think there were only five songs that I wrote by myself. The others were all cowrites or other people's songs. So Jac was still wondering whether I was going to be a writer. So that album kind of convinced him because all the songs, for the exception of one, were songs that I wrote [other] than the Kris Kristofferson song. But I actually helped to write that song, too, 'I've Got to Have You.'"

If the singer-songwriter movement of the early seventies was a hurricane, Simon was at the vortex. And that is something she remembers vividly and fondly, from opening for Stevens to Harry Chapin opening for her. It is her friendship with Stevens, now known as Yusuf Islam, that remains special to her.

"There's still some part of me that's waiting for him to call. And he did call me about fifteen years ago. It was on my birthday and he called. We had a wonderful talk. I said, 'I can't believe you're calling.' But it was just a coincidence that it was on my birthday," she remembers. "And then I saw him ten years ago in London. He just stopped by my hotel just to say hello. And Ben [Taylor, her son] was there. My son was there with me, just doing the dates that we did in London. And Steve sat in my hotel room and Ben played 'How Can I Tell You' for him and it was one of

the most incredible experiences because Ben sings it so beautifully. And then Cat Stevens, he sang something for me and Ben.
And oh, I guess maybe he sang the same thing. Ben sang it and
then Steve sang it."

It is the friendships and relationships from that era that stand
out most to Simon. Remind Simon that she earned her second
of fourteen Grammy nominations for the *Anticipation* album,
and she laughs. "I have no memory of that."

But reminiscing on the artists she played with, she'll tell you
them all. "I went back to the Troubadour twice when I was promoting *Anticipation*. Harry Chapin opened for me and Don Mc-
Lean opened for me. They both opened for me and then I opened
for Kris Kristofferson in that same juncture," she recalls. "So
those were all when 'Anticipation' was the star of my show. That
and 'That's the Way I've Always Heard It Should Be.' [I was]
working on 'You're So Vain.'"

Part of the reason she associates the songs so much with the
songwriters is they are tied together. "We shared songs, we
played songs backstage. That was a great time, especially at the
Bitter End and the clubs downtown," she recalls. "We used to
collect in the greenrooms and backstage rooms and say, 'Hey, I
just learned this new song, you wanna hear it? You wanna hear
this chord I just learned?' There was just a lot of trading, trading
knowledge, and that's what made it so exciting and I think that's
what made it into such a conglomeration. We all were a part of
each other's songwriting."

Simon still feels thankful and fortunate to have been part of
such a golden age of songwriting. "What's so amazing, of course
we didn't know it at the time, and I hope you agree with me, is
that the writers, we of the early seventies, have really lasted," she
says. "It was a time of music that really feels golden and it feels
like we weren't the only ones that agreed with that."

One of the questions for all of the songwriters at that time was how to handle the lucrative, but often controversial, opportunities to have their music placed in commercials. And we are certain Simon consulted with some of her troubadour friends when she was approached by ketchup company Heinz about including "Anticipation" in the ketchup commercial that would become so iconic it was parodied by *Saturday Night Live*. Not surprisingly, Simon says she was hesitant to do the commercial at first.

"I was very reluctant to sell that song to Heinz because I thought that I was too good for that. I thought that was going to be a very lowbrow experience for me. But it was just after Sally was born. It was 1974. It was right after my daughter was born, my first child. And I thought, *I'll never work again. I'll never make another cent.* And I was determined to never live off James [Taylor]. Boy, that's a good thing I decided that," she says. "And so, my wonderful manager, Arlyne Rothberg, convinced me to do it. She said, 'It'll be fun, it'll be camp, we won't do it unless it's funny.'"

Simon, as is the case with all the artists in this book, has several songs that could have been included in this collection. And she does have a lot to say about the lasting impact of her 1989 Oscar-winning song, "Let the River Run," and her working relationship with iconic writer-director Mike Nichols, and of course "You're So Vain."

"Both 'Let the River Run' and 'Coming Around Again' came really easily to me. And I think Mike Nichols was kind of a muse. The amount of energy that I put into pleasing him was subtle enough to me. I didn't realize how strong a presence he was in my life right away," she says. "So when he asked me to write the music for *Heartburn*, which was 'Coming Around Again,' that kind of happened very naturally. I said to Mike, 'What do you think this song is about? It's going to be in the front of the movie and also played during the movie.' And he just thought and he said, 'Again.' So once he said the word *again* to me, I just got 'Coming Around Again.' That's one of my most loved; there's almost nobody that doesn't love that song, that is a fan of mine."

So what was it about Nichols that inspired her so strongly? "Well, you'd have to know Mike to realize that he was so smart. So smart and so funny and so kind. All of those three things. And you just wanted him to love you. Anybody who knew him just wanted Mike's approval more than anybody else's that they knew," she says. "And Mike and I started not really dating but we started seeing each other before we started working together. And anytime he would call, he was just one of these people, he was always going to give you something great every time you talked to him. And I wanted to do the same for him. I wanted to be the same persona for him."

That inspired her to write "Let the River Run," which would garner her an Oscar. "When he asked me to write the song for *Working Girl*, as soon as I saw the script for *Working Girl*, saw the ferry going into the downtown to the World Trade Center. Those buildings were there in the film and in the script for the film, as soon as I read the script, the definition or the explanation of what was going on in that first scene. And I felt myself aboard the Staten Island Ferry, I saw New York as being a jungle. And I wanted to have a jungle beat over a hymn or under a hymn. And it seemed a good match."

In fact, she says there is a common bond between "Anticipation" and "Let the River Run." "I remember the first time playing that for Mike. And boy, those first times, you're just holding, clutching, hoping that they're going to like what you've written. Because it was essentially for them, in the case of 'Anticipation,' for Jac. Jac was going to be responsible for whether the record came out and how much it was promoted. And in the case of the songs I did for Mike's movies, it was going to be Mike who was going to make the decisions about it. And there were some experiences with Mike that weren't so good, that didn't end up so good. But those are forgotten," she says, laughing.

As for "You're So Vain," the song obviously holds a special place in her life's work. "Somehow 'You're So Vain' always seems to have eclipsed everything. And when people come up to me on the streets and they say, 'I love your songs and my favorite one is . . .', it's almost always 'You're So Vain,'" she says. "There's the mystique of who it was written about. And I don't know why that happened. There were other songs that have been about a certain person and there wasn't always that interest into who it was about. I can think of some other songs where people wondered who it was about. But not as many as 'You're So Vain.' People were fascinated."

Given the breadth and scope of her massive catalog, and as stated, that a number of Simon's songs could have been chosen, she was given the option of what song to include. And though she talked about several songs, it was Simon who ultimately selected "Anticipation." Because great artists like Mandy Moore and Dinosaur Jr. front man J Mascis have covered it, because of what the song means to her, and because of the fan connection, which people still tell her on the street to this day.

"The kids that come up to me on the street now are into the music that I wrote for the Disney Piglet movie, *Piglet's Big Movie*. I get a lot of people who listen to that. But there are enough people that say, 'Of course, "Anticipation."' So 'Anticipation' goes in the 'of course' category."

CHAPTER TEN

DON McLEAN

✦ "AMERICAN PIE" ✦

ew songs in history have been as analyzed and scrutinized as closely as Don McLean's 1971 epic opus, the eight-minute-plus "American Pie." The lyrics have literally become the subject matter of college courses, where teachers and students try to dissect who the jester, the king, and the queen are.

McLean says even his fellow artists have wondered about that. "Jakob Dylan came up to me. I saw him at a place, my girlfriend likes him. And he said, 'Okay, you can tell me, Don. Who is the jester?'" McLean says, laughing. "He said, 'My dad's the jester, right?' I said, 'I didn't say that, I never said that.' As I was leaving him—we had a great time with him, he's a terrific guy—I said, 'Well, he would make a good jester though, wouldn't he?'"

But as McLean explains, he would have had no problem calling out artists by name if that's who he was referring to. "What I want to point out is that I mention people by name in that song.

I mention James Dean. If I'd want to mention Dylan instead of the jester, I'd just say Dylan. Or I'd have said Elvis instead of the king," he says. "I meant to do that because I wanted there to be an impressionistic feel to the lyrics rather than being sort of a regular old rock 'n' roll song: 'Here's a song about Chuck Berry' or whatever. So it was a whole different breed of cat which defies discussion of the lyrics. You can't do it. Otherwise you change what the song is supposed to be. That's why I don't do it. Not because I'm trying to be coy or anything."

In discussing the song now, though, McLean hits upon so much of the reason for the continued appeal and mystery of "American Pie." As much as it is a sprawling epic about a decade of musical and cultural history, it works, like all great songs, because McLean took his own personal life and made it universal. So people see themselves in the song.

"The song was very personal. There's a lot of personal references in that song. Like when I say, 'For ten years we've been on our own,' that's me," he explains. "For the ten years, the 1960s until I made my first record, I'd been on my own since my father died. See? So all those magic years when I was learning I perhaps had a [feeling] something was going to happen to me. Those are the ten years that I was on my own and then the song begins, the first verse. But there's a lot of things. I'm watching things and saying what I'm seeing. So I'm on the outside, always. I've always been an outsider."

From the beginning, "American Pie" has been a complicated, complex journey for both McLean and the audience. After all, an eight-and-a-half-minute song chronicling a decade of pop culture history really had no business being a number one smash. So how did it happen?

"The song was immediately edited. They didn't ask me about it either. They edited it down to three minutes. And that's what got to be number one, was the three-minute version of 'American Pie,' backed with 'Vincent.' Or maybe it was 'Castles in the Air,' from the first record," he recalls. "I don't know, they were already getting two albums on the charts at once. Because I had *Tapestry* and *American Pie* probably in the top twenty at the same time. So I think they were cross-branding or something like that. But they, on their own, I never heard a word about this. All of a sudden this short, hot little version of 'American Pie' with the chorus, a couple of verses, and the chorus fading out over and over. That went to number one."

But "American Pie" is just not a song that can be edited. No one wants to see only the trailer of *The Godfather* or *Citizen Kane.* You need the whole story to appreciate the breadth, depth, and scope. What makes "American Pie" special is the complete narrative it weaves. And fans found that quickly.

"Then people bought the album and they heard the song and they called up Top 40 and they said, 'We don't want to hear this thing, we wanna hear the whole song,'" he recalls. "So they took the album into the booth and they had to play that on Top 40 radio, because they didn't have the technology to put eight and a half minutes on one side. And then they released a single with part one and part two. So that's how they dealt with that."

Now, looking back on the song with the perspective of half a century, McLean sees the ascent of "American Pie" to anthem status as the people's will. "The whole thing has been completely, I hate the word *organic*, but I've never had any plan or any power people that have shoved anything down the public's throat. Everything that has come from me has been the people's choice," he says. "When they [the National Endowment for the Arts and the Recording Industry Association of America] did that big list of the greatest songs of the twentieth century, I had a whole lot of people, including the guy running the thing, who were hostile to me. They were not Don McLean fans. So when all of the sudden 'American Pie' kept coming back as top three or four or five positions, they couldn't believe it. So again, the people's choice."

Given the lyrical complexity of the song, though, McLean says it did take a minute, understandably, for fans to catch on to the depth and power of what he conveyed in those eight minutes plus. Recalling early shows playing the song live, he admits it wasn't an instant classic.

"I remember singing at a college in Philadelphia. I was opening at that time. I was still doing a lot of opening for William Morris, all their acts on the road. As well as starring in nightclubs and doing my own college shows," he says. "But there is an artist named Laura Nyro that I liked a lot. And I was really excited about being on her show and hearing her. And so I think I sang it there. And I remember a very underwhelming response, like, 'Okay, what was that?'"

That changed quickly, however, once the song became a radio staple. "Once the album was number one and the single was number one in 1972 and 1971—because it was number one at the end of '71 and the beginning of '72—I was doing one hundred and fifty solo shows a year and selling out every theater and concert hall and nightclub you could imagine," he recalls. "You could imagine people hanging from the rafters, listening to every song from those first two records and of course concluding with 'American Pie.' And there were usually thousands of women, women came from everywhere. Young girls were the primary audience that I had."

That might have been the primary audience, but "American Pie" transcends age, gender, ethnicity. It is one of those songs handed down from generation to generation, and a big part of the magic of the song is McLean's undeniable and obvious love of music. Fans feel his sorrow at the losses of the Big Bopper,

Buddy Holly, and Ritchie Valens on "the day the music died" and they relate. For McLean, that palpable love of rock 'n' roll goes back to his adolescence.

"I go back to hearing 'Heartbreak Hotel' at dusk. It had just turned dark in the summertime on one of those portable radios in the 1950s. 1956 or whatever is was. I was ten or eleven. And hearing that, it was the most powerful experience that I ever had," he recalls. "Nothing ever compared to that, hearing 'Heartbreak Hotel.'"

Like so many artists, McLean explains he turned to music to find where he fit and discover his voice. "I was ill most of the time when I was growing up so I was home with the record player and the radio and the television. And I created a whole fantasy world. It didn't have anything to do with what I was supposed to be taught in school. I created a whole other world in my head with TV, radio, the Top 40, and the records that were laying around the house," he says. "I had a much older sister who was fifteen years older. And so there was a big stack of seventy-eight records. And somehow I'd go through that and always manage to find one I didn't see before. And so I'd hear all this stuff. So I love old-fashioned popular music, too, Ella Fitzgerald and Sinatra and Nat King Cole and all those people. I love old-fashioned show business. But I also was completely involved in the fifties rock 'n' roll thing, and the early sixties. Love the Beatles when they first came around. Still love the Beatles. The brilliance of those records, the harmony, the sense of . . . I don't know, they're perfect."

Talking to McLean is fascinating as you see the direct lineage from his childhood, living in the fantasy world of his music, and creating a whole universe in "American Pie."

"That's why I'm an artist, and not a football coach. I'm an artist for that reason. I knew what I was supposed to do. There was no other way for me, no other thing. When I would hear the records coming over that Victrola, which was a big console with a beautiful, polished mahogany and everything. And big speakers. The speakers were very good in those days. They were huge. And I would just lose myself. I would want to crawl in there, man. So making records was the most exciting thing ever. That was the thing I lived for, was to make records," he says. "The idea for me always was I have to make an album. And I was always pushing for that throughout the sixties. 'How do I do that?' And it was a laborious, painful, never-endingly frustrating thing. But once I did that *Tapestry* album and I held that in my hands in 1970, that was a transformation. I did it. And no one could ever take it away from me."

Nor can anyone ever take away from him the inarguable legacy "American Pie" has had in popular culture. The list of artists who have covered it is a testament to its rock 'n' roll greatness: Jon Bon Jovi, John Mayer, Madonna, Garth Brooks, the Brady Bunch. For five decades the song has endured as a touchstone of popular culture that is instantly recognizable and evokes a flood of emotions.

McLean remembers when it changed over from a hit to an anthem, a song that would without question endure in future generations. "I would say that probably around the time I had a number one of 'Crying,' which was in 1980 or '81. And what happened with that was nothing changed. All they did was play 'American Pie' and 'Vincent' twice as much. And I think that's when it crossed over at that point," he says. "Another thing was when they started calling February 3 the day the music died. I had nothing to do with any of this. Around the time 'Crying' was number one around the world. And it was five in the United States or something like that. That completely surprised everybody. But it didn't change anything. 'American Pie' just got bigger."

Now it is one of the go-to songs for movies and TV. As recently as 2020, forty-nine years after McLean's version hit the top of the charts, it was used brilliantly as the climax of the first season of the Emmy-nominated NBC TV series *Zoey's Extraordinary Playlist*.

The shows and movies that have used "American Pie" are as impressive as the list of artists who have covered it. Netflix's *Stranger Things*; Marvel's *Black Widow* movie; the seminal sitcom *The Office*, starring Steve Carell; and *Charlie Wilson's War*, with Tom Hanks and Julia Roberts.

Ask McLean his favorite, though, and he immediately gravitates to one that united him with a slew of music legends back in 2003. "Yeah, the commercial, which had Prince, me, the Beach Boys, Elton John, all in the same commercial for Chevrolet," he says. "I remember that. I thought that was pretty cool. That was a number of years ago."

He is also a fan of a number of the covers he has heard of the song, starting with John Mayer's version on *The Late Show with David Letterman* in 2015. "I thought it was very good. Bon Jovi was singing it. I just think it's a matter of time before one of those guys realizes all they have to do is go in the studio and record the whole song and they're going to have a massive hit record," he says, pointing out the recent success he had teaming with the a cappella group Home Free.

"This Home Free a cappella group, in Nashville, did an a cappella version of the entire song. And it was a sensation. And it was number one on the country video charts for eight weeks," he says. "This is a big deal. Somebody like John Mayer or Bon Jovi should go in the studio and cut this song. The whole thing. And do it like they know how to do it with the kind of technology and musicianship that they're able to get. And they're going to have something."

They could have another hit with it, just as Madonna did in 2000 when she reached number one in multiple countries, following McLean's chart-topping success twenty-nine years earlier. A great song is a great song, and "American Pie" has proven to be as timeless as baseball and, well, apple pie.

But the legacy of the song is so much bigger than commercial success. "The song has changed the world perhaps. Maybe 'American Pie' has changed people's perception of a lot of things. And put a focus on perhaps Buddy Holly and Ritchie Valens. That it might not have had without the song," McLean says.

CHAPTER ELEVEN

THE SPINNERS

✦ **"I'LL BE AROUND"** ✦

*D*etroit R&B group the Spinners had a whole career before they were introduced to the majority of the world via their 1973 self-titled hit album on Atlantic Records. They had labored on Motown as a middling group, with quality songs, but no substantial commercial success to speak of.

Given their lack of commercial popularity, Motown assigned the members to be chauffeurs, road managers, and chaperones, and to do other odd touring jobs to justify their place on the label.

At the suggestion of a fellow Detroit artist, Aretha Franklin, who was signed to Atlantic, the group left Motown for Atlantic and a fresh start. And they found it at Atlantic right away.

"We were working with Atlantic Records. And the man that was the head of it, and in charge of the Spinners project, he was a good friend. So we kind of felt special," Henry Fambrough, the last original member of the group, says.

So when the vocal quintet teamed with songwriter-producer Thom Bell for their Atlantic debut it felt like both a creative rebirth and a reason for optimism. "We didn't know. But as they say we were hoping and praying," Fambrough says, laughing. "Thom Bell with his track record, we kind of figured it would be kind of good."

To call the end result of Bell and the Spinners teaming up "kind of good" is like saying the pairing of Marvin Gaye and Tammi Terrell was not bad, or that Paul Simon and Art Garfunkel had a few hits. The union of Bell and the Spinners took the group from being respected but largely unknown to one of the biggest R&B acts in music throughout the seventies.

The self-titled album spawned five Billboard Hot 100 singles, including two top ten songs. And it all began with "I'll Be Around," which went on to platinum status as their first million-selling single.

Funnily enough, the song began as the B side to the single "How Could I Let You Get Away." But the power, reach, and appeal of "I'll Be Around" was immediately undeniable, as Fambrough recalls. He says it was a hit right away, with radio onboard from the get-go.

"We started listening to it on the radio. And the announcer kept saying, 'This is the Spinners' new song. I think they did it right this time!'" he says. "I think about that still."

It's understandable that after so many years of waiting for success, Fambrough can remember every detail of the group finally getting the support of their label and radio, and how that felt as he realized the group was on its way to a long overdue hit single.

"I heard it in the car. When I was switching channels and stuff, it was already playing," he recalls, still as enthused as if he had just heard it on radio for the first time yesterday. "When it was over they announced, 'That was the Spinners and their new single. Anybody that likes it, call in and let me know how you feel.' So that's the first time I heard it on the radio."

Fambrough got a special treat too. Being on a promo tour he got to talk directly with fans who were falling in love with the song. "That happened when we were at the radio station," he says. "People were calling the station while we was on the air talking to them and they would call in, he would tell them to call in and they could speak to one of the Spinners. They would call in and we would talk to the fans. And that was great."

You can still hear when you talk to Fambrough nearly fifty years later how much fun he had every step of the way in promoting "I'll Be Around," as it rose to its eventual peak of number three on the Billboard Hot 100, number one on the Billboard Soul Singles chart, and number one on the Cash Box Top 100.

For instance, when he talks about performing the song on *The Midnight Special* in 1973, that was a joy for him. But, as he says, every time they got to play the song live was a blast.

"Every time we did it, it was a memorable performance," he says. "[But] the most defining moment was, when you're doing like *American Bandstand*. When you're doing shows like that. *Midnight Special*, doing a show like that. And you got the audience there . . . everything stands out. Because it's like you're doing it for the first time. It's almost like this is your first record, you know what I mean? Sometimes it feels like that."

He remembers every detail of that *Midnight Special* appearance. "That was the number one show on the weekend. It was a live performance there when they were taping it. And they had the kids there, they had the audience there so it was just like doing a show," he says. "When you're doing a live TV show with an audience, you got a guy standing on the side telling people when to clap, when not to clap, and how loud to be. So that's how that works on the TV thing."

For Fambrough the TV and radio appearances stand out because he was excited to interact with the fans and hear their reactions to meeting with and talking to the Spinners.

"We did the TV shows and they had the live audience there. And the kids, the way they responded to it. And on the radio, when we do the radio shows, they would have a chance to call in," he recalls. "And he would sometimes, whoever we were visiting at the station, sometimes they would play just a little bit of the original. Then they would say, 'This is the Spinners. And this is the latest version of this song.' They would play it, and then the phone would start lighting up."

When he talks about the latest version, he is referring to the 1995 rap hit version of the same name. The song, by Rappin' 4-Tay, sampled the Spinners and brought the track back to the American charts, hitting number thirty-nine on the Billboard Hot 100. That same year, the Spinners' original was featured in the hit film *Dead Presidents*.

The song has definitely enjoyed a strong second life via covers and movies and TV. The artists who have chosen to cover "I'll Be Around" speaks volumes about the song's cross-generational and universal appeal. Hall & Oates, who also appear in this book, have done it. As have the Afghan Whigs—one of rock's most underrated acts—Joan Osborne, Freddie Jackson, and superstar Seal.

The song, through samples and covers, has appeared on the charts several times, including Terri Wells's version, which hit the UK charts; a new wave version from the band What Is This?, produced by Todd Rundgren, charted on the Hot 100; and the rap group TRU, featuring Master P, hit the top ten on the Hot

Rap Songs chart with the song "Tru Homies," which sampled "I'll Be Around."

It's enjoyed an equally prolific life in film and TV. In addition to *Dead Presidents*, the song was used in the popular sitcom *My Name Is Earl*, the 50 Cent film *Get Rich or Die Tryin'*, the TV version of *Lethal Weapon*, the hit series *Cold Case*, ABC's *Private Practice*, the FOX animated series *The Cleveland Show*, and most recently on the smash HBO series *Big Little Lies*, starring Reese Witherspoon and Nicole Kidman.

The cover versions, and especially the samples in rap songs, and being used in series like *The Cleveland Show*, have introduced the song to younger generations. Fambrough gets such joy from talking to kids who have become the new era of Spinners fans because of "I'll Be Around."

"When you're touring or you're visiting the station and they play it and everything just jumps at you. And you're so happy with it and you're listening to the people when they talk to you. And you can hear the excitement in their voice and listen to how they talk and how they talk about the Spinners and the song that they love that we're doing and they're so happy that we're doing this particular song," he says. "The younger generation, if we get a chance to speak to them, they always say, 'It's a song that we love' and everything. One time, I think a little girl stood up and she said, 'I really love this song here. Thank you!' Stuff like that."

Hearing those stories takes Fambrough back to the song's origins, when the Spinners were first out on the road introducing the song to fans. "We were promoting the song. It had just come out. It had just been released, and we were promoting in the city where we were working in—and that's how that works. We was doing, what they used to call it, a 'round-the-block thing," he says, laughing.

Then when the song became a hit they got to experience the audiences' fervor for hearing the song live. "We opened the show with it for a long time. It was that good," he says. "And the people that were there at the time, you could see it, the excitement in their face and how they cheer for the song and how they cheer for the Spinners. And see how everything was going. Everything was great at the time."

The period of greatness culminated with the song hitting number one on the Cash Box chart, an incredible moment for Fambrough after so many years of reading the magazine and seeing others ascend to the top position.

"I used to read the *Cash Box* magazine and look at where the song was setting at the time," he recalls. "And what made us so happy about it, looking at *Cash Box* and reading it and seeing our song, the Spinners being number one on top. That was so good."

When the song was at its peak popularity, riding the top of the charts, Fambrough and the rest of the band were on the music industry hamster wheel of fame and having a hit song, so they didn't get the proper opportunity to celebrate having a number one song.

"At the time we were still touring. And we were working in a different city just about every other night," he says. "So we were just enjoying it, and the people that we were performing for, they started requesting it, 'Sing this song, sing it.' I remember the people being so excited about it. And that felt good, that felt really good."

Of course, the reward for all that hard work is that half a century later, they get to still reap the benefits of the song's success and timeless popularity through stories of how the song has influenced and impacted the lives of the fans who've grown up with "I'll Be Around."

"We heard a lot of stories about the song. And I remember one time we was doing an interview and a lady stood up and said, 'That song played at my mother and father's wedding. That was the first time we heard it and we love it,'" he recalls. "So stories like that, it goes on. It's really great."

Having played the song for nearly fifty years and listened and watched the fans' response to the song, Fambrough understands why the song resonates so deeply with fans then and now.

"Even the title of the song stands out. And so, when you're listening to it, especially when you're performing onstage with it, and the people are down front and sing along with you, it's self-explanatory," he says. "The song, it speaks for itself."

CHAPTER TWELVE

BARRY MANILOW

✦ "COULD IT BE MAGIC" ✦

*B*arry Manilow has sold over eighty-five million albums worldwide, had eleven top ten singles on the Billboard Hot 100, including three number ones, and was anointed as next by none other than the Chairman of the Board himself, Frank Sinatra.

Yet Manilow never had aspirations of pop stardom. "I had no intention of becoming a performer or singer or any of that; I had no desire to become a solo singer or performer or anything," he says. "I was just writing. Hoping that everybody else would record my songs."

One of those songs, "Could It Be Magic," was recorded by other people, and it changed the trajectory of his life and career forever. For him it was the 1976 Donna Summer version that breathed new life into a song that, if it were a cat, would have been on at least life three.

The song's incredible journey from obscurity to timeless standard starts with life one. "I wrote 'Could It Be Magic' and Tony Orlando was producing a song that one of my collaborators was writing. When I wrote 'Could It Be Magic,' he said, 'Why don't you do the vocal on this one too as Featherbed [an early band featuring Manilow]?' I said, 'Sure, I'll try it,'" Manilow recalls. "So he went into the studio to record my beautiful ballad called 'Could It Be Magic.' I had written it, I thought it was going to be this beautiful ballad the way I heard it in my head. And I got to the recording studio and he had done an up-tempo version of 'Could It Be Magic.' I thought he had ruined my song because in my head it was going to be this magnificent ballad that builds and builds and builds. But he took it and he made it into 'Knock Three Times' or 'Tie a Yellow Ribbon Round the Ole Oak Tree.' Here was 'Could It Be Magic' sounding like 'Knock Three Times' and I just kind of walked away being very unhappy with it."

Although he hated it then, Manilow admits today that time has been much kinder to the Tony Orlando–produced version of the song. "Now years later I play his rendition of it and it's just a great record. It's a great rendition of 'Could It Be Magic,'" he says.

As much as he, being the writer and artist, thought Orlando ruined the song, it led to Manilow's first record contract. "Then after he did that, I ridiculously got a record contract. It was ridiculous. I never thought about singing," he says. "But Bell Records offered me a record contract because of those two songs that people like my voice on. And so I made a record and I put 'Could It Be Magic' on my first album."

As a solo artist whose name was now at the forefront, Manilow could finally realize his vision for "Could It Be Magic." "[It was] the way I always heard it, which was a big ballad that started small and ended huge and it was eight minutes long and nobody had made an eight-minute song, maybe the Beatles. They'd done everything," he says. "And people liked it on that first album. That first album sold five copies but the people who bought it loved 'Could It Be Magic.' Then that first album disappeared."

So now at this point the song has had two of its nine lives, as an up-tempo, Tony Orlando–produced track and the epic version that Manilow had in mind when he first wrote the song.

But it was, as the cliché goes, the third time that was the charm. "Out of the blue I got a phone call about a year later from a guy that ran Casablanca Records, Neil Bogart," Manilow recalls. "So he called and said, 'You gotta get up here, you gotta hear this. Donna Summer's done "Could It Be Magic."' So I run up to Neil Bogart's office and they play it for me and I loved it. I loved what Giorgio Moroder and Donna did to 'Could It Be Magic' and that was the one that did become popular. They do know 'Could It Be Magic' as that rendition. And since then, there've been various vocal groups that have discovered 'Could It Be Magic' and they do, especially in Britain, they're always good. The vocal group versions of that are great."

Today, the Summer version stands as one of his two favorite versions of the song, which has been recorded around the world in several languages. "There are two. There's Donna's. Who did a perfect up-tempo song. Frankly, the Take That, that is a pretty damn good rendition of that song. It really is. Somebody was really in charge of that one. Because they kept everything about the song and made it their own. So those are the two," he says. "[That's] including my first record. When I go back, I didn't know anything about making records and I listen to that and I say, 'Good for you, that you could do something like that.' Young guy who didn't have any experience in a recording booth. And to make a record like that. And it still holds up. That one and the other two. Donna Summer and Giorgio. I think it was Donna's idea to do 'Could It Be Magic' and then Giorgio Moroder added his magic to it. And then, like I say, Take That, I was thrilled. And I saw them do an a cappella version of it. And they did it great a cappella. It's very difficult to do with that song. No instruments, just them singing 'Could It Be Magic.' With all of those complicated chord changes and they did it beautifully."

Even before Summer resurrected the song, he had known it was something special from the way audiences responded to "Could It Be Magic" live when he was still working with Bette Midler.

"I used to work with Bette Midler. I was her music director and her arranger and her piano player. In the early, early days," he says. "And she exploded on the first tour and on the second tour, by that time I had made my first album and I was stuck. Do I go on the road? Bell Records wanted me to go on the road to promote my first album. Do I go back to Bette who's relying on me for her big tour? So I made a deal with Bette that I would continue to be her music director, but in between act one and act two, would she allow me to sing three songs from the new album? I mean this was crazy because I had never performed anywhere. Anywhere! And I was asking her to perform in front of her five-thousand-person audience. Five thousand people every night. She was huge. But I didn't know how I could get away from promoting an album on a small tour of my own or leave her. And I didn't want to leave her. She and her manager said okay. They let me do three songs opening her second act. It was crazy. I'd never been more nervous in my life. And I had three songs from my first album that I chose to sing for the audience. I played two songs from the album and then I played 'Could It Be Magic.' And every night it brought the house down. Every night. They shouldn't have done that. They were waiting for Bette to come back and they should have not been friendly or listening. But they liked the first two songs. But they loved 'Could It Be Magic' from the very first time."

There is one performance of the song from those first times performing while on the road with Midler that stands out to Manilow. "That Bette Midler tour, when I got to the Red Rocks in Denver, I'd never seen anything like that," he says. "And Bette finished her first act and she was not going over well because they could not hear her. She couldn't connect. And it's huge, in the middle of a mountain. She was having a really bad time. And I went out there and thought, *This is going to be dreadful.* After I finished 'Could It Be Magic,' I saw people standing up and I thought they were running, they were running to get out. But they were giving me a standing ovation. And it was the first standing ovation I ever had. And it was because of 'Could It Be Magic.'"

Reflecting all these years later, Manilow is still humbled by that standing ovation. "I really thought they were running for the arches. And they should have been," he says. "They came to see this fantastic performer. What's the piano player–conductor doing keeping us away from her? But they were great. They were supportive. Bette's audience were very supportive."

While that first standing ovation is a career highlight for Manilow, that is not the only performance of "Could It Be Magic" that he remembers fondly. "Carnegie Hall was great. I opened with 'Could It Be Magic' at Carnegie Hall. It was just at that particular show. I came out in white tie and tails," he says, laughing. "I flipped my tails and sat at the piano and played the Chopin prelude. It was very nice."

For Manilow, every time he talks about "Could It Be Magic," from the writing to the success to the iconic live performances, it comes back to the Chopin opening for him. That's where the writing began, as he tells it.

"The way I wrote it was after a glass of wine, I was playing my Chopin, which I do now and then because that's where all the melodies come from. And I left the piano and played around for a while. And then I came back and I wrote 'Could It Be Magic' and I realized that I was ripping off the Chopin chord change that I had just played," he says. "Every musician that plays 'Could It Be Magic,' they swoon on those chord changes because they're just so beautiful. And I based the song on those chord changes."

Those chord changes particularly resonated with Manilow's fellow musicians. Summer, Take That, and Leona Lewis have all have covered the song, proving Manilow was spot-on in his belief he had crafted something that would endure with "Could It Be Magic."

"I knew I was onto something. Sometimes you just know it. It came so fast; the ones that come fast I know that I have something going. The ones that I struggle with never work. But the ones that come fast, something's in it. All I could tell you was that I loved this song," he says. "And I loved producing it for myself with Ron Dante. And it was exactly the way I had imagined it. And I listen to it, and it's a billion years old and it still holds up for me because it's so inventive that it does exactly what I want it to do. I'd never heard a song like that."

"Could It Be Magic" is just one example for him of it meaning he has something when a song comes to him immediately. "When I have to struggle with it, I think the listener can hear the struggle and it just doesn't work," he says. "There's a song I wrote for the *2:00 AM Paradise Café* album with lyrics from the late Johnny Mercer, 'When October Goes.' It's one of his lyrics. I put the lyric on the piano and hit the keyboard. I just read the lyric, played it in one take. Same thing with 'Copacabana' by the way. One take, I hit the cassette machine and I read the lyric that Bruce [Sussman] wrote and I just played it and then shut the cassette machine off. I never went back to it and that was 'Copacabana.' Those are the ones, for me, that work and the ones that I have to go back over and change this, change that—they never work for me."

The most memorable example for him, though? "It was the song called 'One Voice.' That one I wrote in a dream. How about that? It woke me up. I tiptoed down the hallway from my room because the rest of the house was sleeping," he says. "And I whispered the song into the cassette machine. Melody and lyric. Melody and lyric! And then I went back to sleep and then when I played it the next morning, there it was, 'One Voice.' And I don't know how these things happen."

As Manilow points out, he has an incredible wealth of love songs, with "Could It Be Magic" being right at the top of the list for his fans, the Fanilows. "I've had a lot of love songs and so the letters that come in are about 'Could It Be Magic' and 'Mandy' and 'Can't Smile Without You,' and 'Even Now,'" he says. "I've just been a lucky guy. I've got an incredible catalog and I get letters over the years about that. And 'Could It Be Magic' is just one of the ones people write about."

Of all those iconic songs, which have been favorites at weddings over the years, maybe none of them have led to as many new lives as "Could It Be Magic," he points out proudly.

"'Could It Be Magic' is a passionate song. I always described it as a musical orgasm because that's what I wanted. It starts small and then gets crazy and then gets calm at the end," he says. "So yes, I've had letters about 'Could It Be Magic' and [people] having children to 'Could It Be Magic.' Thanking me. I always feel like I'm there. I like being involved. I always feel like I'm a part of the family."

It's funny because, as he has mentioned, it wasn't his plan to be a performer. "I never, ever expected to go through anything like that. Because like I said, I had no desire to be a performer live at all. I was very happy in the background. Arranging music and conducting and playing the piano. That was really going to be my life," he says. "I did a lot of commercials, orchestrating them. I had ten years of a career that was about to really explode. I would have wound up in some, I don't know, Broadway orchestra pit conducting for *The King And I* or something. That would have been just great. But fate had a different story for me. I wasn't supposed to be in an orchestra pit, I was supposed to be making people feel good. And that was the beginning. That second act."

In many respects, it all comes from "Could It Be Magic." "It's the one that holds up for me out of all the ones that I've written. And of all the ones of the outside material that I've recorded. That's the one that I think I'm the most proud of," he says. "Like I said, it's the first one that came so easily. And I'm glad that I found that great prelude. And I think, like I told you, when musicians play it, they swoon, they just swoon. That's the one that musicians will remember me for."

CHAPTER THIRTEEN

KISS

✦ **"ROCK AND ROLL ALL NITE"** ✦

O f all the songs in this book, KISS's 1975 song "Rock and Roll All Nite," off the band's *Dressed to Kill* album, is the only one that started out with the goal of becoming an anthem.

"Interestingly, the seeds and the germination of 'Rock and Roll All Nite,' the start of it, was actually Neil Bogart, the president of Casablanca Records, the label we were signed to in the seventies," Paul Stanley recalls. "He brought us into his office and he said, 'You guys need an anthem.' That was not a word that was used at that point. He said, 'You need a song that your fans can rally behind and kind of embodies what you are and what you believe, like Sly and the Family Stone have, "I Want to Take You Higher" or "Dance to the Music."'"

So with the directions of his label president in mind, Stanley began the Herculean, near-impossible task of trying to write a song that would last for the ages with the orders of writing a timeless classic. I say Herculean because pretty much any artist will tell you that when you are trying to write a hit, 90 percent of the time or more, you will fail miserably. Great songs often come by accident, by inspiration, by luck, or when you least expect them. But Stanley had his marching orders from Bogart.

"I remember going, 'Ah, okay.' And I went back to the hotel, which was the Hyatt on Sunset, picked up my guitar, and pretty quickly came up with 'I wanna rock and roll all nite and party every day,' as a chant with the chords underneath it," he recalls. "I went to Gene [Simmons]'s room, knocked on his door, and said, 'Listen to this.' He said, 'I have a song called "Drive Me Wild."' And as fate would have it the two meshed together and became 'Rock and Roll All Nite.'"

Though Stanley had been instructed to write an anthem, and had come up with one that would one day be voted the sixteenth greatest hard rock song of all time by VH1 and the twenty-sixth greatest rock song by *Ultimate Classic Rock*, and would consistently place near the top of classic rock radio station countdowns of the greatest rock songs of all time, the song was not an immediate sensation. Though it did become an immediate favorite with their live audiences.

"Yes, they did respond to it right away," he says. "You just have to remember that at that point we were not playing for large crowds. We weren't a headliner playing large arenas. Other than Detroit and Cobo Hall we were still either second on the bill or headlining theaters. So yes, the whole audience would sing 'Rock And Roll All Nite,' but we hadn't sold a lot of albums. For example, *Dressed to Kill*, at its height, probably sold about one hundred and twenty thousand albums, which back then was not even quite mediocre. So it took the live version to, I think, pull people in to the idea that there were crowds, or was a crowd, singing the chorus. Yeah, it went over big with our audience, but our audience wasn't big."

So what was the turning point, where "Rock and Roll All Nite" went from being a fan favorite for a small, but devoted, audience to a recognized anthem? To a song that would be universally acknowledged as one of the great rock 'n' roll party songs of all time? A song that would be covered fifty times by artists as diverse as Green Day, Van Halen, Poison, L.A. Guns, Samantha Fox, Toad the Wet Sprocket, Happy Nite Quartet, and countless more? A song that would become a favorite in movies and TV, in such diverse works as the Bryan Cranston film *Why Him?*; Martin Scorsese's Bob Dylan Netflix film, *Rolling Thunder Revue*; the Amazon Prime series *The Dangerous Book for Boys*; *Lip Sync Battle*; the popular sitcom *Dharma & Greg*; and on and on?

The song has become so ubiquitous and versatile in pop culture, as a symbol of fun, frivolity, freedom, and rebellion, that it has been used in the beloved family sitcom *Full House*. And it's also been used in the classic Richard Linklater seventies-themed film *Dazed and Confused*. And performed at the MTV Video Music Awards in 1996 and featured on the hugely popular sitcom *Family Guy*. "Rock and Roll All Nite" is much bigger than one song. It is an emblem—one that signifies teenage freedom and defiance.

But when did that transformation start to occur? According to Stanley it was when the song became a live favorite and KISS evolved from a band on the brink of stardom to a Rock & Roll Hall of Fame act that has sold over 100 million albums worldwide and headlined stadiums around the globe.

"When we recorded it for *Dressed to Kill*, it really didn't take off. It was probably too simple. And not to draw any kind of comparison, but let's just say in a sense, although we share little in common musically, [Peter] Frampton had loads of songs that didn't come alive until *Frampton Comes Alive!*" Stanley points out. "And 'Rock and Roll All Nite' didn't become 'Rock and Roll All Nite' until it was on *Alive!* And then it reached the multitudes, reached the magnitude that it could be an anthem, a rock anthem. And it really became the template for other bands trying to replicate that. And it was the rallying cry, it was a quick synopsis of what the band was about and what the fans wanted. The simplicity of 'rock and roll all night and party every day.'"

Though the term *party* in the seventies, and even today, has a heavy drug connotation, Stanley wasn't implying that at all, a point that makes total sense when you consider that Simmons has denounced drug use throughout his entire career. To Stanley it was just about enjoying life, helping reiterate once again why the song has become one of the most beloved and joyous party anthems of all time.

"Partying, for me, had nothing to do with drugs. To me partying meant celebrating life, having a great time, being at a party," he says. "Once it was on *Alive!* it just exploded. I think the fact that people would hear the live version and hear an audience singing along made people feel like, 'Well, I want to be part of that audience. I want to be part of that KISS nation.' So it took people hearing that to consequently make a bigger audience."

Even Stanley is pleasantly blown away by how the song overcame its modest start and has grown into its mythological stature as KISS's signature song, no small feat for a band with a catalog that includes "Detroit Rock City," "Beth," "Calling Dr. Love," "I Was Made for Lovin' You," "Strutter," "Hard Luck Woman," "Lick It Up," and countless more hits.

But when KISS headlined a New Year's Eve livestream in 2020 and the subject of the closing song came up, Stanley almost laughed at the idea of any other track ringing in midnight. "I think 'Rock and Roll All Nite' says it all. So I would say that is the song," he says.

He goes back to the song's origins to look at the incredible transformation "Rock and Roll All Nite" has had in the annals of the KISS story. "Certainly with 'Rock and Roll All Nite' it's amazing over the decades how it's resonated and only built in stature. And I remember sitting in a hotel room on Sunset Boulevard and coming up with the chorus. So that's the power of music," he says. "And the stories associated with the creation of songs or how they became well-known is fascinating. It's not lost on me and yes, when we're rehearsing, I go, 'Wow, we're KISS and these songs are great.' When we start 'Detroit Rock City,' I go, 'Wow, this is potent stuff.'"

It is a testament to the song's impact and Stanley's memory that more than forty-five years after the song was initially released on *Dressed to Kill* he vividly remembers many of the details from the song's genesis, from the meeting with Neil Bogart and the writing of it at the Hyatt on Sunset to the first time the band played it in the studio.

"I think the first time we played it live so to speak was in the studio when we did *Dressed to Kill*, the third album. We brought the song in and showed Peter [Criss] and Ace [Frehley], who would usually come in," he says. "We would go in the morning and polish up, Gene and I would go in and finish songs. And then Gene and I would have Ace and Peter come in and we would say, 'Today's song is called "Rock and Roll All Nite."' And we would run down the song and then record them."

Now, more than four decades later, the song's place in the set list as the closing track is secured. The KISS Army know that as the band's legendary spectacle comes to a close each night, as the pyrotechnics and all the highlights of the show that have made KISS a top draw for decades wind down, the night will end with the frenzy and sing-along of "Rock and Roll All Nite." And every time they play it, according to Stanley, it's just as special as the night before.

"Every night we play the song. As corny as it may seem, every night we play the song is a validation, a vindication, and a celebration of everything we've accomplished. It ends the show for a reason. It kind of puts the bow on the package, it symbolizes a wrap-up of everything we accomplished," he says. "So every night when we play it I have that same feeling of what we've accomplished and looking out at a multigeneration, a three-generation crowd, singing it. And singing it with smiles on their faces because we did it together. The song immediately elicits a reaction. Because if you're one of the older fans it takes you back to a moment in time. It's like a soundtrack to the life you had or were living. And for younger fans, maybe it's a recognition of joining something that has a long and powerful history."

That, in particular, is special for Stanley, seeing the kids not even born in 1975 scream every word. Just like "(I Can't Get No) Satisfaction" by the Rolling Stones, "Hey Jude" by the Beatles, and "Baba O'Riley" by the Who, "Rock and Roll All Nite" has become a rite of passage passed on from grandparents to parents to kids. Watch a KISS concert and you see the joy as generations wrap their arms around each other and scream that mantra in unison: "I wanna rock and roll all nite and party every day."

For Stanley, after all these years, it leaves him speechless. "It may be cliché, but it sometimes can bring tears to my eyes, choke me up. Because a great song goes beyond the literal lyric; it becomes a representation for something so much more," he says. "So when you have an audience singing, 'I wanna rock and roll all nite and party every day,' they've attached their own individual meaning to the song. And that's palpable. So when I see multi-generations singing it, or people in other countries singing it, it's overwhelming sometimes because the song has a meaning to those people that may go far beyond the simplicity of the lyrics. It's what they've attached to the lyric."

CHAPTER FOURTEEN

JANIS IAN

✦ "AT SEVENTEEN" ✦

Janis Ian wrote the 1975 smash "At Seventeen" for teenage outcasts everywhere. The song became an immediate hit by reaching out to everyone who had ever felt alienated, left out, bullied, or just like they didn't fit in.

But Ian learned early on, while on tour in 1975, that part of the song's popularity was that everyone, regardless of how their social status appeared, could unfortunately identify with the song's themes.

"I had a really great lesson on the road about that. With 'At Seventeen' at its height I was playing somewhere. It was a relatively large hall, about seventy-five hundred, and at that point in a career you're always meeting the mayor or the local dignitaries and their families. They're all brought backstage to meet you before the show or after," she recalls. "And someone came backstage with quite literally the prom queen and prom king from that year. And he was also the football star. And I looked at these golden people, tall and blond, just American-hero looking, and I said to the boy, 'What could you possibly find to relate to in this song? You must have a date every Friday night.' And he said, 'Yeah, and imagine how people talk if I don't.' That was a real eye-opener for me because I had never understood the most popular kids were also terrified and worried about losing their popularity."

Ian wrote the song when she was only twenty-three (the song appeared on the 1975 album *Between the Lines*, which came out just before her twenty-fourth birthday), so not far out of her teens herself she still had a lot to learn. And the song and its universal popularity taught her a lot in a short time. For starters, there was the fact that men related to the song as well.

"They responded right away," she says of the live audiences for the song. "It was one of the interesting things about that song because I was on the road with it before I went on the road with the record, so I'd probably been playing it around six months maybe before it got recorded, and the audience reaction had always been really positive. And then what blew me away about it was the reaction was positive for the men as well as the women. That was surprising to me."

Though Ian was taken aback, in a good way, by the song reaching across genders, she knew instantly the song was a hit. "I called my manager at the time and said, 'I think I've just written my first hit song,'" she recalls. "That's one of the few times in my life when I absolutely knew that without a doubt. That's a very rare thing. But I just knew it the minute I finished the song. Then it was just a question of making sure that people like my former manager didn't get in the way of the song. But they left me alone to make the record with Brooks [Arthur, producer]."

Left to her own devices, Ian knew exactly how she wanted the song to sound and feel. So, as she explains it, with just her and Arthur at the helm, it was a smooth recording process.

"I knew what I wanted to hear. That song is very much based around, or the recording at least, is based around the guitar part. The guitar part is a fundamental part of it. So the guitar part pretty much dictated where the recording would go. It'd have to be a samba feel, it'd have to have that airiness and lightness, it had to stay out of the way of the lyric, which is always difficult for certain musicians," she says. "And it still had to have that indefinable thing Brooks Arthur brought to it, which was an insistence that every bar feel as live and alive as the bar before it. So when we recorded it, it probably took about three hours I think."

When Ian says she and Arthur were at the helm, she is not exaggerating. According to her, part of the reason the session took as long as three hours was dealing with musician egos.

"Part of that time was just wasted because I had invited a young guitarist, who had never done anything professional before, but was very hungry to. And I had invited him as rhythm guitarist, or one of them. And there was a fairly big-shot studio player on the session who was supposed to be lead. And he was so mean to this kid that I threw him off the session because he felt the amateur, as he put it, had no business being on the session," she recalls. "Whether we ever even heard this kid's playing, I wanted his excitement because I felt like that would generate in the room and it did."

She and Brooks knew exactly what they were looking for, which meant though the song took hours, the vocal sessions were much more time-consuming and intricate. Now she is thankful he pushed her the way he did.

"The vocal to 'At Seventeen,' though, took three days. And that was because we only had one track left. And Brooks was insistent that it be alive in every syllable. And I didn't have the command of a microphone or the voice I have now. In fact, I learned a lot of it from Brooks," she says. "So it took me a lot longer than it would have now, I think. Brooks was absolutely right though because when you listen to that vocal, it's alive every second. And it's sincere every second. It reeks of truthfulness, which is pretty amazing for that long a song from start to finish."

Having written a song so deeply vulnerable and personal, Ian wasn't going to let the recording stray far from her vision. She was determined to stick to what she wanted.

"It's hard when you can't get it right. Everybody gets stomachaches and it becomes really frustrating," she says. "That's one of the reasons I taught myself to orchestrate. I was tired of having to go through another person to explain myself."

She knew it was a hit. What about other people? "Brooks knew it was a hit. He had no doubt. My manager at the time knew it could be a hit, but she wasn't sure that I wasn't blowing it. And I know that the promotion people at Sony, what was then CBS, believed it was a hit record. So there was a lot of faith in the record. It was just conquering the people who didn't have that faith," she says.

Since this was back in 1975, they were allowed to get creative with the promotion and marketing. "So Herb Gart, who was the executive producer on that album, did a couple of very smart things that would probably be illegal right now. He took out radio ads, or had CBS do it, where the song played for forty-five seconds, and then fifteen seconds for voice-over to say '"At Seventeen" by Janis Ian, from the album, *Between the Lines*,'" she says. "So by the time that forty-five seconds had elapsed, people were already into the song. The programmers for television wouldn't touch it. It was too long for morning TV for the housewives. So he sent copies to every program director's wife he could find. And he did the same with a lot of the AM stations. And the wives then said, 'This is a great song. Oh my God, this is my life.' And got them to play it."

As Ian points out, the song, though it hit number three on the Billboard Hot 100 and was nominated for multiple Grammys, including Song and Record of the Year, as well as won for Best Female Pop Vocal Performance, was not an immediate, out-of-the-gate hit. "Then I was on the road for probably six months before it really gained any traction with all of the might of CBS behind me," she says. "It was such a long-duration hit. It didn't have the wham, bam of something that raced up the charts to number one. People shared it a lot with each other. People sang it a lot to each other. But it wasn't a number one hit. It was just like 'Society's Child' in that respect. Once a certain area of the country went on it, another area would think, 'Okay, maybe I'll play it.' And then when the first area dropped off, the second area would suddenly go on it. So it stayed on the charts for a while, it sold a lot."

Ian also believes that because she was so synonymous with the song, that is one of the reasons why people were initially reluctant to cover the song for years. It wasn't until the late nineties, almost twenty-five years after the song's release, that it became popular for artists like Céline Dion and Jann Arden to put their own unique spins on the deeply personal tale.

"I think the reason it wasn't recorded at all in those early years was because it was so identified with me because it was so closely identified with my voice and that presentation that the only two cuts it got were Stan Getz and Hugh Masekela. Both were instrumentals," she says. "I think people were really afraid of it. It would be like somebody recording [Barbra] Streisand's 'People.' It's so identified with her voice that it's really dangerous because everybody is going to be going, 'Oh, that's not as good.' 'Oh, that's better.' Like it's a contest or something."

She is a big fan, though, of artists covering the song, starting with Arden's version, which she remembers hearing first. "I know that the first outside recording that I heard was Jann Arden's in Canada. And there hadn't really been any covers of note until Jann. And she did a bang-up job of it," she says.

Dion's version also struck a deep chord with Ian. "Céline Dion did an amazingly good job on it. I love her version. I think it's an honest, straightforward, no gimmickry, no tricks, nothing but her own experience. And she really brought it to the song in a way that most artists can't," she says. "Another reason why I think I like Céline's version so much, and Babyface too as producer. They made a commitment to the song itself that, for me, shines through when she sings it. Or in the record anyway."

The one time Ian saw Dion perform it live she was just as impressed with her interpretation of the song onstage as she was with the record. "We only heard her do it live once. It was pretty spectacular that once," she says. "We were in Nashville and Céline was playing in Nashville. And we were invited to the show with four friends. Really, she was just wonderful to us. She actually held the show ten minutes so we could go backstage and say hello before. She was just really lovely to talk to and to deal with. I think she and Bette Midler may be the most gracious people I know among performers. Then we watched her do the song from the seats and it was amazing. It was really wonderful. It was like when I first saw Bette do 'Some People's Lives' and she didn't know I was in the audience. As a writer, what I'm looking for is artists who do a great job on my song. And it doesn't have to be a Céline Dion or Bette Midler; it can be a Joe Blow. It doesn't really matter. But if they do a great job then I'm honored."

During that brief introduction before the Nashville performance, Dion told Ian the story of how she came to do "At Seventeen" and why the song quickly came to mean so much to her.

"She had been presented with the song by the former head of the Grammys, the television Grammys, and her husband, as a song that they thought would help her transition from Céline Dion, the rock 'em, sock 'em pyro person, to Céline Dion, the more mature artist. And they felt that doing 'At Seventeen' would really be a hallmark for the shows and for the album. That's why they featured it on the Grammys that year," Ian recalls. "She was very clear that the moment she saw the lyric and heard it and read it, it became her song. She was very clear that the song was about her childhood. That speaks to the universality."

At the time of this interview, August 2021, Ian said, "I've always thought of myself as a writer first. I'm seventy and I've been a songwriter for fifty-eight years now."

As a writer, one of her primary goals was to write a song that resonated around the world with everyone. "I've always wanted to write universally. I've always wanted to write songs that anyone from any culture could understand. I think my best songs speak to the universal," she says.

It took several years, she says, for "At Seventeen" to connect around the world the way it did in the States, but she saw a shift around the turn of the twenty-first century.

"One of the interesting things about 'At Seventeen' these last fifteen years is that it was never a hit anywhere but the United States, not even close. And when I would go to the UK or Japan I would have to sing my local hit," she explains. "And then about fifteen years ago, maybe twelve years ago, I went to Japan and for the first time everybody knew that song. And for the first time there was applause when I started playing it. And the same thing happened in the UK a few years earlier. And in Ireland, and in Belgium and Holland. So all of a sudden the song took on its own life in a different way than it had had a life before. It became part of the universal library of music, not just the United States. And that, to me, is the greatest thing about it because that shows that I did my job. I hit the universal and it went into all of those people's hearts."

Though Ian can't say for sure what prompted the late-blooming, global popularity of "At Seventeen," she does have some theories on the song's more recent acceptance in other countries.

"I can guess that people's mothers were playing it for them, people's sisters were playing it for them, people's brothers were giving it to them. I could guess that but I really have no idea," she says. "I think that 'At Seventeen' is still relevant because, as my acting teacher Stella Adler says, it speaks to a truth. And the truth doesn't change. I think that it became relevant in Japan, I think part of it is Americans were traditionally more willing to bare their hearts or, conversely, to bleed all over everyone than most other cultures. We're a much younger country. I know in Japan, when I first went there in the seventies, women were still giggling behind their hands. They never showed you a smile. And no one would dream of admitting they were having a problem with anything. It was just not in the culture [in the] UK, stiff upper lip. So to embrace that song as a culture means that the culture itself had to change."

Another likely reason for the song's global ascent is that it's a massive part of popular culture. For starters, the song has a huge place in history, which Ian chuckles about now. But she was the first musical guest ever on *Saturday Night Live*, in October 1975. Though now that makes her a part of pop culture history, she had no idea the show would still be on five decades later. It was another gig, and not an easy one because she admits that early performances of the song were difficult for her.

"It's a hard song to sing, it's a hard song to perform because it's brutally honest," she says. "There is no escaping that song. You can't sing that song without getting involved with it. At least I've never found anybody who could."

Since that October 1975 performance the song has been utilized countless times in movies and TV. Tina Fey used it in both *Mean Girls* and *30 Rock*. It's also had four different placements on *The Simpsons*, as well as in movies such as *Teaching Mrs. Tingle* and *Blood Ties*.

There is one use in film and TV that stands out most to Ian. To her, it was by far her favorite. "I thought the way they used it in the six-part English series *The End of the F***ing World* was absolutely brilliant. It brought me to tears. It was one of the best uses of 'At Seventeen' I've ever seen, just astonishing," she says. "I actually asked Sony/ATV to put me in touch with the writers and the music directors so I could thank them directly. They were lovely. I think that those people are not contacted very often by artists and it means a lot when the artist thanks you. I know it means a lot to me when an artist thanks me. So how much more must it mean to someone who loves music to the point that they would become a music supervisor? They were really happy about it. And it was a great usage, oh my God."

Over the last five decades Ian has seen her baby grow from a song she knew would be a hit into a global anthem that touches people deeply. And she has had so many stories from people about what the song means to them.

"Fans certainly tell me things like that and it's certainly important to them that they thank me. And that's a great part of it," she says.

After listening to those tales for so many years she does understand why the song resonates so deeply with fans. For starters, it is her vulnerability in the lyrics and vocals.

"In 'At Seventeen,' I think there's a sense of safety because it's someone else singing it," she says. "So to take what other people feel and are afraid about and don't want to talk about it because it's humiliating, and to give it a voice that's someone else's voice allows people to connect in a way that perhaps they find difficult when it's only them."

Then there is another aspect to her that speaks so directly to fans: it offers hope for everyone who feels they have no chance at escaping their isolation, loneliness, or persecution.

"I think part of the charm of 'At Seventeen' is that there's a happy ending. The assumption is that the ugly duckling will become a swan," she says.

CHAPTER FIFTEEN

HALL & OATES

✦ "SARA SMILE" ✦

One of the keys to a song becoming timeless is that people can hear themselves and feel their own stories in there. For instance, John Lennon obviously composed the Beatles' "In My Life" with someone or some personal experience in mind. But it became a classic because everyone who fell in love with the song, or to the song, has that one person they think of in their life they love more.

That is certainly the case for Hall & Oates's "Sara Smile," a song as intimate and personal as any in this anthology. Daryl Hall wrote it for his then live-in girlfriend, songwriter Sara Allen, whom he has talked about openly over the years.

"I was sitting in my apartment in New York City, and living with Sara Allen. And I just sat down on the piano—she wasn't there—I just sat down on the piano and started playing, and wrote it," he recalls. "And I don't remember, actually why I wrote it, I mean as far as what was the catalyst. Might have been a fight, might not have been, might just have been a feeling of, 'Okay, everything's okay.' But I was just sort of describing life as I saw it at the time where I felt it, and I just wrote down exactly what I felt. And that was it. There it was. The song was written very quickly; I didn't mull over it or anything like that. I came up with the chords, then I came up with the lyrics almost simultaneously, and there it was."

Very similarly to Graham Nash's "Our House," "Sara Smile" paints a picture of intimacy and vulnerability. With the soulful ballad Hall takes you into his home, into his relationship, giving you a glimpse into his life and how he felt being in love at that time. It could have been a painting, a photograph, a short story. It's an invitation into his partnership with Allen.

That is so much of the appeal of the song, that it invites you in and allows you to, as stated, see yourself, or what it is you long for in the three-plus minutes he shares with listeners. Some writers might have an issue being that open, but Hall says that has never been an obstacle for him.

"I don't have a problem with being vulnerable. I'm not afraid to say exactly how I feel and show how I feel. That's something I've done more than once and many times actually in my songs," he explains. "But as you say, the one that probably everybody would focus on the most would be 'Sara Smile,' at least so far anyway. Another thing about this song is it represents continuity, it's you and me forever. It's not just an 'I love you and you love me' kind of thing. It's about, whatever happens, if you wanna be leaving, you can go. Every word means something in that song. It's like you could be loose. You could be far away. We could stay away from each other for a long time, none of that matters. Whatever the feeling is, it's beyond all that. And I think maybe that's something that people relate to."

Whatever it was that people related to or found in the song, Hall says he saw it in the response from live audiences immediately.

"I could tell you when I started playing it live, it immediately became the cornerstone of the whole show and it still is. It's never changed. I sort of look at it like [Paul] McCartney's 'Yesterday.' Everybody is waiting for that song to happen through the show, then it happens and there's like a collective sigh in the room, and I look at the crowd, I can see their faces, I can see what they do," he says. "They get this sort of a glow in their eyes and it's an amazing feeling, really. But I felt this from when I first started performing it. It wasn't a hit at first, it was sort of unknown. Then it became an R&B hit. It was our third single that we released, but we were doing it even before it was a hit and people were responding to it that way. So, even though I was surprised that it finally became a hit, I knew that it was moving people from the very beginning."

One show that gave him an early indicator of the song's deep resonance with listeners was when the duo were performing in the UK. For Hall, seeing the normally stoic audiences there unable to hide their feelings still resonates with him almost fifty years later.

"I remember when I first started singing, we started touring in the UK really early, in 1975. And I remember singing that song to a British audience," he recalls. "And I remember seeing the British, who are notorious for not wanting to be sentimental at least on the face of things, react to that song in a way that was uncharacteristic of the British audience, and they continued to do that. And so, that was something I noticed from the very beginning, and still do notice."

For Hall, from the beginning, the song has been special live, one that not only was the centerpiece for the fans but also for him as the singer. "I used to use it as a jumping-off point for everything. It's a soul song, really, and I'm a soul singer at heart. And I used to go and do all kinds of vocal, whatever I felt like. Just a spontaneous series of ad libs and impromptu ad hoc things," he says. "And I used that song, I used to stretch that song sometimes ten to fifteen minutes and just singing whatever came into my head. And like I said, I don't do that as much as I used to, but that seemed to be something that people related to. And that became, at the time anyway, the showpiece of the set, when I would do those kinds of things."

Though the song was an immediate live favorite, Hall is not exaggerating when he says it wasn't a hit right away. The song hit its peak position of number four on the Billboard Hot 100 the week of June 26, 1976, ten months after the album's August 18, 1975, release.

Hall can still remember hearing it on the radio, months after its release. "I do remember, I was in LA, and I remember it 'cause I don't listen to the radio very much. But I heard it on whatever pop radio station was in the car," he says. "And my first reaction to it was it doesn't sound anything like any of the other songs that are being played right now. It was completely out of context. And I thought, *Wow, well, that's either good or bad. But in this case, it's good.*"

A look at the top ten the week "Sara Smile" reached its peak confirms Hall's assertion. Surrounding the tender soulfulness of "Sara Smile" was the pop of Paul McCartney and Wings' "Silly Love Songs," the sugary pop of Captain & Tennille's "Shop Around," and disco favorites such as Silver Convention's "Get Up and Boogie" and Starland Vocal Band's very much of-the-times ode to midday sex, "Afternoon Delight."

Given the prevailing tides on pop radio at the time—jovial, playful, upbeat, even a little frivolous—Hall's surprise his little love song eventually wound its way onto radio and the charts is

totally understandable. Then as he explains, the song has continued to pleasantly amaze him.

"Like many of my songs, a lot of them are really personal, but
they take a life of their own once they leave my hands. And I
think 'Sara Smile' surprised me, to tell you the truth, of the different things that people have done with it. The rap artists and
everything, of course. And the different ways that it was used. I
never would have predicted that."

Some of the ways are more obvious. For instance, the song has
been covered countless times, by artists such as Boyz II Men,
Joan Osborne, After 7, Eric Benét, the Bird and the Bee, Gary
Clark Jr., and many more. While Hall is flattered by those, he
admits he is far more drawn to those artists who take his original
vision and pull it in a different direction.

"Covers are fine. People want to cover my song, that's good.
They'll do it their way, hopefully," he says. "[But] adapting it,
they're using it to do something different and not just repeating
it. I did one with a guy named B-Legit, where I sang the chorus.
I sang a version of the chorus called the 'Ghetto Smile,' and he
rapped over it. And that's what I did with him. And that was a
remake of the song. And there's been a number of those kind of
things that I found interesting. And sometimes like, that I listen
to and liked. That matters to me, for the cover versions."

It's also, like all of these songs, transcended generations
through its use in movies and TV. Just as the way the song has
been adapted into rap, for example, pleasantly surprised Hall, the
range of films and TV shows the song has been in is incredibly
wide.

It's been in the Christian Bale and Mark Wahlberg film *The
Fighter* and the brilliant John Cusack and Kate Beckinsale romantic comedy *Serendipity*, and sung by two of the main characters in the TV cartoon *The Boondocks*, based on the popular

comic strip. But there is one use that stands out above all others: the song was played while the beloved characters of TV's massive hit *The Office* looked at photo albums in the series finale. The final episode of a show like *The Office*, which in 2020 was the most streamed series by more than eighteen billion minutes than the runner-up, *Grey's Anatomy*, almost a decade after it went off the air, ensures that the song will continue to find new audiences year after year.

Hall sees the influx of new listeners every year he and musical collaborator John Oates are on the road, selling out venues around the world. "Yeah, that happens to me all the time. Most of my audiences weren't born when that song was written," he says. "For a while now, I feel that I have sort of crossed the generational line into some other thing. I'm not just an icon to my contemporaries or whatever you want to say; people tell me that their kids like me. It's universal music. It transcends time and space."

Of course it doesn't hurt the song's popularity with younger generations that it feels like one out of every ten kids was named after the song. Hall jokes about how many times people come up to him and have said they were named after the song. "Millions, I can't tell you how many people. Well, not millions, obviously.

"Unusually, back then, the name Sara, especially without an *H*, was a less-than-common name. I didn't know very many people named Sara. It seems like now there's so many people named Sara, it's ridiculous," he says with a chuckle. "But in those days, it wasn't really that common a name. And I used it, obviously, that's her name. And then I truly believe that I sparked something, a whole generation of people naming their kids Sara."

He's heard a few personal tales about the song being directly responsible for the name Sara. "Somebody just said to me the other day that 'I was named after that song,' and she was a middle-aged lady, whatever. And then not that long ago, somebody said, 'I just named my newborn baby after Sara,'" he says. "It never stopped, this whole thing. People that were born in 1975. My cousin named her daughter Sara, because she was carrying her at a concert in her body, and she felt her starting to move around when I started singing 'Sara Smile,' so she called her daughter Sara. So I have a niece named Sara; that's the way it goes. It happens so often. Sarah Ferguson, the Duchess of York. She told me that when she was a kid they used to sing 'Sara Smile' to her all the time."

Those are perfect examples of how such a personal song written about a specific woman in a particular moment of time has become a big part of other people's lives and stories.

Talking about songs from other artists he admires for their candor, Hall goes back to John Lennon. "Probably some of John Lennon's songs were that way, 'cause he was very intimate with himself," he says. "Todd Rundgren, he's my contemporary but he writes that way sometimes. The song 'Can We Still Be Friends' is a very poignant song. And I know he meant it when he wrote it. There are two right there."

But few can match the detail Hall offers in "Sara Smile." "It was really one of the most straightforward, focused songs I've ever written. I always said it was just like a postcard. And it's all absolutely real. Was real and, still to some degree, is real today," he says.

When he says it is still somewhat real today, he is referring to the fact that he and Allen broke up in 2001, after a more-than-thirty-year relationship. But, as he explains, the song still carries many of the same emotions for him when he plays it live today.

"I sing it onstage and I still feel it. I don't even necessarily feel the feelings about Sara, the subject. I feel it about the concept," he says. "People just relate to it, they've always related to it, I still relate to it."

When watching audiences sing along to the song, Hall notices how the song transports them to a different time and place. "It just brings everything down to a place. When you're at the [Hollywood] Bowl, look around you and you'll see what I'm talking about. It's the way people react to it because it's so real," he says. "It's intimate, it's about continuity, it's about the ups and downs of life. It's an emotional life in a nutshell. I'm proud of it."

He is particularly proud of the song and how it has been recognized as being a soul song, which is how he intended it to be heard. Hall & Oates made the Rock & Roll Hall of Fame and became the biggest-selling duo of all time based on their "blue-eyed soul" sound, and that all started with "Sara Smile," their first top ten hit.

So when he hears from people how the song's soulfulness moved them, he is incredibly touched. "It isn't about what they say particularly about it, it's just that they acknowledge it, the Black community in particular. Whenever I bump into people on the street or in situations that there's a different kind of take on things, it definitely moves people in the soul," he says. "And it's that more than anything. I don't even notice any specific thing anybody says like, 'I really like that lyric or this or that about it.' It just moves them. The whole piece moves them."

CHAPTER SIXTEEN

AEROSMITH

✦ "WALK THIS WAY" ✦

*A*erosmith's "Walk This Way" became a rock anthem in the seventies. But to guitarist Joe Perry, it was never a straight rock song—it was a funk song.

"When I wrote the music in Hawaii at that sound check, I was really into the Meters and into funk," he recalls. "And Joey [Kramer, drummer], because he played in a Temptations cover band and he played in our band, had kind of a couple of funky beats. So I thought, *Why try and cover something funky like a Sly and the Family Stone song? Why not try and do our own?* So that was the thing. I said, 'Just play a straight, straight, straight beat, okay?' And with that, I wrote all the riffs of the song. So 'Walk This Way' was kind of like my attempt to bring that funk side that we knew we had. But to do it and make it our own."

Now, of all of Aerosmith's many iconic anthems—including "Sweet Emotion" and "Dream On," among others—Perry feels that "Walk This Way" is the one best suited for this book because the song and its place in history have changed so much over the years.

"'Walk This Way' is the one I have to say has had the most evolution over the years," he says. "Because it had kind of a different kind of vibe for a band that they didn't know what to call us. A heavy metal band? Or a rock 'n' roll band? Or a poor man's Rolling Stones. Nobody knew what to say about us. So it just hit the mark for what I wanted to do."

That said, Perry admits when he first started writing the song, he had no idea that it would go on to be both a rock and later a rap anthem, with Run-DMC, more than forty years later. "No, not any more than any other song," he says when asked if he knew the song was special. "We were at the point when we had to write in the studio. And this is true of a lot of bands. They get in the studio for the first time and they're playing songs that they've been playing for, I don't know, however long they've been together and written them. Because they've been playing in clubs and trying to make an impression and get some fans. And, back then, you did it by playing live. And you knew pretty quick if the songs were gonna work. I mean, if you played a song and people didn't really respond to the song but they love when you covered 'Honky Tonk Woman,' you know it's time to write something else. But we didn't know it was going to be something different."

So did those early club audiences respond to "Walk This Way" immediately? As he remembers it now, the answer is yes: it did become a crowd favorite fairly quickly, even if it wasn't exactly instantaneous.

"I knew 'Walk This Way' had that beat. I'm sure when people first heard it, they would have rather heard 'Toys in the Attic' or 'Back in the Saddle,' 'Same Old Song and Dance,' because it was easier to identify with as far as getting up and dancing and moving," he says. "But 'Walk This Way' started to be a song that we could start the set with or end the set with. Because it got people up. And they stopped trying to figure out what it was and realized they could move to it. That was the most important thing. Again, that was back in the era when these songs had to entertain a live audience. If it didn't get played on the radio right away you had to convey that feeling in a live situation. And 'Walk This Way' did it."

Perry had an epiphany of sorts about the song and rock in general just in the last few years. And it comes from an unlikely source for Aerosmith. "I remember Dick Clark, on his show there, *American Bandstand*, he would run down the top ten and it was like, 'Can you dance to it?' Well that really didn't resonate with me until last week, I don't know. Seriously in the last couple of years," he says.

Looking back now on "Walk This Way," he feels it was the first Aerosmith song to capture that *Bandstand* vibe that Dick Clark would have so appreciated. "It's the vibe and the tempo and the beat, which is, to me, the heart and soul of the song. Obviously words and the melodies and all that evolve, like the key. But every fucking song on the radio, all in the history of rock 'n' roll, relies on the beat and the tempo," he says.

"Walk This Way" did hit the top ten, peaking at number ten on the Billboard Hot 100 in 1977. But Perry has no recollection of that, saying the band didn't care about radio or charts.

"At one point we got a list from somebody in the late seventies of all the singles. I'm not even sure it was then. Maybe it was into the eighties after I came back. Of all the singles, of all the songs that had been released as singles. And the numbers of how far up they got. There must have been twelve songs. Some of them made it into the thirties. And we had no idea what songs got on the top ten or the top twenty. We just didn't follow that shit," he says. "We were so involved with playing to the audience and see-ing the reaction. And I remember the early years, we'd sit in dressing rooms and sometimes you could hear people leaving the clubs. And you'd hear them laughing after a show. Laughing and breaking bottles and singing some of the songs. And we'd know we'd done a good show. We didn't know what songs were being released as singles. We didn't listen to the radio. It wasn't really our thing. So no, we were totally not cognizant of that whole top ten thing. We never tried to write songs for that. We just wrote songs because we thought that they would have the dynamics to excite people live."

Though the song hit the top ten in the States and became a staple of FM radio, Perry doesn't remember the song being a hit until they rerecorded it with Run-DMC in 1986.

In his estimation, it probably was that funk beat he was going for that appealed to them. "And I think maybe that's what the rappers heard when Run-DMC got hooked into that beat and it worked for them. It wasn't that it was so fast. It was just that it had a vibe," he says. "And the riff I guess. And when we recorded it with them, I know they changed the lyrics a little bit. And so it was obviously about the feel and the melody and the chorus."

But it was the collaboration with Run-DMC that shifted the song's trajectory from a rock anthem to a trailblazing pop culture milestone. And even though Aerosmith was one of the biggest rock bands in the world, he noticed the song opened doors around the globe.

"I really don't remember it being a big single or anything like that until this whole Run-DMC thing happened. And a lot of people didn't know the band existed until that single. Especially in Europe. We were blown away," he says. "We were hearing peo-ple go, 'Wow, this is great. Do you guys have any other records?' It was really like, *holy shit*."

The comments still bring him a chuckle all these years later. "After it came out, and the video came out, and I have to say, every time a fan would come up and they would say, 'Wow, do you guys have any other records?' And this is after the seventies, and they'd never heard of us in Europe. So many fans, they were too young or just we didn't get on the radio, we weren't big in Europe yet," he says. "We never went back as many times as we should've. I wish we'd have played in Europe more. We only went to Japan twice I think. We should have been playing over there a lot more, especially in Europe. So a lot of people thought it was our first record. And I have to say, I get such a laugh out of that. And I know why, because we weren't that big, in Europe. Until 'Walk This Way' with Run-DMC. Those kind of comments are very entertaining to me."

Of course the version with Run-DMC was pioneering, possibly the first rap-rock hybrid, and it came along at the time of MTV, which, as Perry points out, changed everything.

"I was told that it was one of the first Black rap videos on MTV. I don't know how true that is, but I'll take that any day. If I can wave that flag I'm fucking proud of that. Are you kidding?" he says. Even he admits he is not sure how true that is, but even the possibility is something he is immensely proud of.

"Not just collaboration, but the fact that they're Black, Black rappers got to be on TV. I mean if it wasn't there before 'Walk This Way,' that's pretty heavy," he says. "I've heard a few things like that, and you hear them and you go, I don't know. This is before Wikipedia or whatever. So I don't know. Maybe it was but if that was even going around in the business, I'm really proud of that."

One thing he is 100 percent certain of is the incredible live performances he got to be part of with Run-DMC. As Aerosmith grew into their eventual Rock & Roll Hall of Fame status and unlikely MTV stars in the late eighties and early nineties, there were some incredible opportunities to perform historic versions of the song.

"There was MTV 'best of' whatever. There were so many of those kinds of shows. And then the Grammys or whatever. I can't remember which ones we played. But after we did it with Run-DMC, I know we got more requests to do it with them if we could do it," he says. "And I know we've had them come up onstage just because they were at the show. And it was great to have them come up; it was like you can't beat that. But I know that we did one show, in Miami, I think the Beastie Boys were on the bill, and Steven [Tyler] and I sat in and their audience knew who we were. It was really cool. But this is after it had come out and the video, which was almost as important as our collaboration in the studio."

He is very clear on the history-making Super Bowl performance with Britney Spears, *NSYNC, Mary J. Blige, and Nelly. He remembers in vivid detail everything that went into that performance and how that changed the Super Bowl halftime show forever.

"There were a lot of firsts on that one too. We insisted that fans be allowed on the field. That never happened before. This was the first Super Bowl [halftime show]that was produced by MTV, or more importantly, somebody other than Disney. Because until then Super Bowl things were . . . they used Super Trouper spotlights. There were no lights on the field. There were no fans on the field. There were a lot of things that just didn't happen before that show. But when MTV came on, they knew how to take it up to the next level. And we said, 'Listen we gotta have an audience around the stage. Bottom line.' We're live performers," he recalls. "And so they came to a meeting of the minds and figured out how not to damage the field. They put tarps down, or plywood, but they allowed fans to come out on the field. The guy who produced some of the biggest live shows like U2 or the Stones, the big stadium shows, he was called on to produce it and everything had to fit into roll boxes that were ten feet long and six feet high. And they had to figure out to get lights onstage, like a real rock 'n' roll show. Colored lights and all that in addition to the spot lasers and stuff and get it done in fifteen minutes. Because you only have fifteen minutes of commercials to set the whole thing up. It was an amazing thing that they did and it was the first time they did it, at the Super Bowl. They raised the thing a whole other level. And since then, now it's like standard procedure. There's fans on the stage, there's fans on the floor. There's fans everywhere, there's spotlights everywhere. The NFL realized they had to move it up a whole notch to make the Super Bowl thing what it is, or what it was. And move it up. So there were a lot of firsts there that people were probably unaware of. That's what I remember about it. And we were standing right next to the football players. Because the halftime show is only, what, fifteen or twenty minutes long? And the football players are all ready to go out and play again. And they're all standing there like gladiators, next to us. And we're like these little rock 'n' rollers compared to them. I mean, they're fucking giants. It was an amazing event and also working with, I think there was *NSYNC and Britney. I'm not sure. But to play 'Walk This Way' out there, that was pretty amazing."

As Perry looks back on the song it's not just the funk origins that stand out to him. It's the song's playfulness. After all, the lyrics were conceived after watching Mel Brooks's *Young Frankenstein* film in Times Square.

"That song, no I did not know what it was going to be. I knew it was a real tongue-in-cheek kind of vibe. Like after seeing that comedy movie. Which fucking everybody was cracking up about to put that in there. It was almost to me a gimmick song," he says. "Jumping back to the tongue-in-cheek thing about a lot of the songs. Aerosmith really has a sense of humor. 'Dude (Looks Like a Lady),' a lot of our stuff has that tongue-in-cheek thing because it's fun. And we didn't try to get into political stuff; we've got some serious songs in there and Steven really blew it away with some great lyrics. But it's really about the melody, depends what kind of road you want to go down with your band. If you wanna be a band that speaks for your generation and all that stuff. All we wanted to do was write songs that people got off on and had a good time and that was it."

Perry is modest about his role in the song. But he is grateful and proud of how the song has endured and evolved so much over the years. "Then of course it carried on, that little germ of an idea about hooking into that funk vibe. For what it's worth, whatever it is, that little bolt of lightning, certainly wasn't that big, at least at that time. But it was enough and I just thank the powers that be that are bigger than me to have dropped that on me, man," he says. "And left it to entertain so many people and make them feel good. And thank you, and thanks for that. And thank the fans for hearing whatever they heard."

CHAPTER SEVENTEEN

BOB MARLEY

✦ "ONE LOVE/ ✦
PEOPLE GET READY"

*T*he number of artists who could have a greatest hits album named *Legend* and not seem arrogant can be counted on one hand. Whoever you argue can be included among those five, there is simply no debate that late Jamaican reggae star Bob Marley is at the top of that short, exclusive list.

You can make the case that Marley, who tragically died of cancer in 1981 at the age of thirty-six, is the biggest global music superstar in the world, even forty years after his death. His music is a rite of passage shared around the globe by kids of all ages, races, ethnicities, and languages. There is a reason that *Legend* is only the second album ever, after Pink Floyd's eternal *The Dark*

Side of the Moon, to spend more than five hundred weeks on the Billboard 200 album charts.

Since the album's release in 1984, three years after Marley's death, the album has spent more than thirteen years on the top 200, and would have been on there much longer if not for a rule that for some time placed it on the catalog charts. As of August 2021, the album had spent 692 weeks on the top 200 and 991 weeks on the UK album chart, a record. All on the way to selling more than 33 million copies worldwide.

What makes *Legend* so special is that it is the best of one of the greatest and most influential artists of all time. From the opening track, "Is This Love," through the closing "Jamming," all fourteen songs are inarguable classics.

Whether it's the timeless tale of nostalgia, "No Woman No Cry," or the always-relevant protest songs, "Redemption Song" and "Get Up, Stand Up," every song has its own special place in history.

So of all of Marley's classics, which have traveled the world moving music fans from Shepard Fairey and Tom Morello to Annie Lennox and Public Enemy's Chuck D, how do you pick one as being the most special?

It may seem impossible, but for one of those who knows best, there is a song that might be Marley's anthem of anthems, the signature song. "'One Love.' Love is the answer to all of these issues. It is love for humanity, love for the environment, love is the universal cure for all of these things, our world being in some of these positions we're in," Stephen Marley says.

Stephen is uniquely positioned to speak about the significance of "One Love." He, like his siblings Ziggy, Damian, Cedella, and Sharon (whom Bob Marley adopted), have all carried on the Marley family legacy with successful music careers. And Stephen, like Ziggy, has frequently performed his father's music live.

So he has seen firsthand the impact and influence of "One Love" on fans, some of whom weren't even born when his father died, seeing the song live for the first time. Stephen, who performed a livestream of his father's music in 2020 as part of the yearlong global celebration of the elder Marley's seventy-fifth birthday, sees "One Love" as a perfect closing song in concert. "For live shows those are closing songs. Those are perfect songs to send people on their way and a message, 'One love, one teacher,'" he says.

Stephen is hardly alone in placing "One Love" at the top of Bob Marley's storied and eternal catalog. The great Carlos Santana calls "One Love" one of the great protest songs of all time, alongside John Coltrane's "A Love Supreme" and John Lennon's "Imagine."[1]

Another person who knows Bob Marley's music uniquely, intimately, and personally is Aston Barrett Jr. of the Wailers. Barrett Jr. is the son of Aston Barrett, who played bass for the Wailers when they backed Bob Marley. Barrett Sr. not only played bass but also was a coproducer, engineer, and musical arranger on several Marley albums, including *Exodus* (*Time* magazine's Album of the Century), the 1977 album that featured the medley of "One Love" and Curtis Mayfield's "People Get Ready."

So Barrett Jr. is well positioned to speak on Bob Marley's music. And he concurs with Stephen and the BBC, who named "One Love" the song of the century—that's right, song of the century, beating out every Beatles, Elvis, Dylan, Stones, and Zeppelin song. Beating "Bohemian Rhapsody," "What a Wonderful World," and "Johnny B. Goode."

For Barrett Jr. it is the message. "The most dominant song of all would be 'One Love,' Bob Marley," he says. "'One Love,' because that's what we need, that's what we preach and we live 'cause it's the universal language of the world. What we all need because we all go through things in life. 'One Love' is not preaching; we're just saying it's always good to be good and be one love, to feel good with everyone."

That message has resonated with musicians for more than half a century. The song has become a unique part of popular culture, from use in the movie *Marley & Me* and Jamaica tourist commercials since 1994 to the countless cover versions by the likes of Jason Mraz, the cast of the TV show *Glee*, Gipsy Kings, Antonio Banderas on the soundtrack of *Shrek Forever After*, and more.

I feel very confident in saying "One Love" is the only song in this book to have inspired a Ben & Jerry's ice cream flavor. At the time the ice cream was announced I spoke with Ziggy Marley and Jerry Greenfield, the Jerry of Ben & Jerry's, who explained why they named the ice cream flavor after this song.

"This message of One Love is more important, more relevant than ever. The idea of people being together, love and social justice, it's needed more than ever," Greenfield said, echoing Barrett Jr.'s sentiment about the power and positivity of the song's message.

For Ziggy, the message is one that cannot be denied. "They cannot stop it, they cannot stop the positive, they cannot stop it. They try and they try and try, but One Love Ben & Jerry ice cream, they cannot stop it," he said, laughing.[2]

That message, and the potency, positivity, and universality of it, is something that Stephen admittedly didn't pick up on until later in his life. Stephen was only nine when his father died, so he didn't grasp how influential his father was worldwide until later.

"After he passed and the relevance of him just became obviously more urgent because his physical presence is not with you anymore. So that's when you really kind of get into the songs. You kind of take it for granted, 'He's around, he's Pops,'" Stephen says. "But without his presence, now it's a different outlook. So I think after he passed away I think all of those songs became like, 'Wow, I didn't even realize that's what he was saying.'"

That is especially true of "One Love," which was first recorded by the Wailers in 1965, then rerecorded and included on the *Exodus* album with Mayfield's "People Get Ready" a dozen years later.

"'There are two versions of 'One Love.' There's an older version— I knew it from the older version," Stephen says. "I always knew it was my dad, but I never knew the song would have such a meaning, such a universal meaning that carries through. That's what I never realized, like, 'Wow, this song is going to be that type of an anthem.'"

But now that he's older and understands how influential the song is, he appreciates it so much more. For example, he embraces all the various covers and those that celebrate his father's music. "I wouldn't say I have a favorite one," he says of the covers. "I'm enthused about all of them. It's like, 'Wow, that was great.'"

But more important to him than the covers and the accolades, as great as those are, is how the song continues to uplift and inspire. Though "Redemption Song" and "Get Up, Stand Up" are the more recognized protest songs from Marley's repertoire, the message of "One Love" carries its own unique brand of power. After all, there is a reason Santana chose it as one of the most important protest songs of all time. And nothing makes Stephen prouder than knowing his dad's song is lifting up new generations of people fighting for right.

"Even some of the protests that have been going on I've heard them break out 'One Love' and all of these things," he says excitedly. "That's just like, 'Wow, look at how significant this man's words and music and outlook is.' It becomes so relevant."

CHAPTER EIGHTEEN

EARTH, WIND & FIRE

✦ "SEPTEMBER" ✦

&arth, Wind & Fire's "September" has become one of the definitive anthems of celebration around the globe. The song's joyous, infectious, upbeat grooves and feel-good tone have made it an absolute essential of countless weddings, bar mitzvahs, quinceañeras, and New Year's Eve soirees. Proving that music truly is universal, the song was played at both the 2008 Democratic and Republican National Conventions. Yep, though they can't agree on anything anymore, even both major US political parties can attest to the fact that "September" is the ultimate jam.

Basically, anytime there is a gathering with a DJ and a big dance floor, you can count on people of all ages, races, and nationalities hitting that floor the second those memorable opening notes come bounding out of the sound system.

Verdine White, bassist for EWF, as they are known, can attest to the song's continued popularity on the party circuit. "It resonates with weddings and things like that. When you go to weddings, you know you're going to hear it," White says. "I've been to quite a few weddings when they start playing it. Or people tell me, 'We're going to play this at our wedding.' Or when I go to the gym, 'My wife and I got married on September 21.' I get those kind of things."

Sometimes, it goes even further than that. "Women are trying to have their kids born on September 21 and things like that," he says, laughing. "It's just something, I think, that caught on."

The song's rapturous appeal and ability to bring people together extends from intimate family gatherings to global celebrations, having become an anthem at sporting events around the world.

Most notably, the song was adapted in 2018 by English soccer fans, who changed the lyrics to commemorate the team's World Cup run. A YouTube video called "SouthGetter" finds such lyrics as, "Hey hey hey/Woah, England are in Russia/Whoa, drinking all your vodka/Whoa, England's gonna go all the way!" And the line, "As we danced in the night" in the second verse gets changed to "And we cheered in the night."

The song's surprising run as a sports anthem didn't start until well after its November 1978 release. However, that isn't unusual, as White points out. "Don't forget now that sports and music are very closely aligned. When you go to basketball games and things like that they're playing music," he says. "But don't forget, at that time when 'September' came out, they didn't play popular music at basketball games or sporting events. Now, of course if you go to any game they're playing the hot records that are out. The hot, the old ones, because it's an entertainment show."

Like so many of the anthems in this book, "September" started under much more inauspicious circumstances. "'September' was basically a filler song on *The Best of Earth, Wind & Fire, Vol. 1* while we were working on the *I Am* record," White recalls. "See, it was in between records. And we put out the *Greatest Hits Vol. 1* because we needed to give CBS a record, an album. So we did that. And it was a new tune on that album."

Looking back on the recording session, which White says he believes was at Hollywood Sounds, he and his bandmates had no idea they had crafted a song that would become so influential and popular it would make people plan their wedding dates around it the same way people plan a wedding around their dream location.

"We knew it was good, but you don't have any idea it's gonna turn out the way it turned out," he says. "And a song like that, it's been a hit like, three, four times, right? We recorded it in the late seventies, and then it became a hit again in the eighties, and the nineties. But you don't know. You go in with the best intentions for all songs, for anything you might do. But you don't know. It's just one of those songs. We call it the gift that keeps on giving."

Though they couldn't have any idea how big the song would become, White recalls they did develop a quick inkling the song would become a hit. "I think we played it on a Friday night and everybody was pretty tired. And I don't think we heard it because I think we were really tired. But then the next day, we heard it the next day and said, 'Well this is a smash.'"

Though the song took years to achieve anthem status, as is typical, the recording itself was fairly straight-ahead and direct as White recalls. "It was basically a lick, groove that Al McKay came up with and Al always came up with great grooves like that, 'Best of My Love,' things like that," White says. "He was always the Groovemaster, we call him."

Although the band knew it was good, and the song became an immediate hit upon its 1978 release as a single—hitting number one on the Billboard Hot Soul charts, number eight on the Billboard Hot 100, and number three on the UK singles chart—as White remembers things, it took the song a minute to become part of the EWF live set, and years before it became the closing staple it has become.

That was because the band already had several hits under their belt, and the song, intended only as a sort of bonus track on the first greatest hits, had to compete with the other already well-established hits for space in the band's popular live show and catalog.

"It was good but don't forget we had other songs then. Like 'Shining Star,' at the time, things like that. 'After the Love Has Gone,'" he says. "It wasn't one of the main songs in the repertoire at the time. It was a nice song, but we had other songs. 'Evil,' things like that. We didn't really get into it until later. It wasn't that it had nothing to do with the song, it's just we had so many other songs."

That first greatest hits collection still features two of the band's most identifiable signature songs, "Shining Star" and "After the Love Has Gone," as well as EWF favorites like "Reasons" and "Can't Hide Love." Then the band went on to have several hits after that album, including "Fantasy," "Boogie Wonderland," "Let's Groove," and more.

So when did "September" start to differentiate itself from the rest of the catalog and pull away from the pack? "Way later, nineties," White says. "Don't forget the song caught fire, because of movies and commercials and things like that that it was in."

The song has been a frequent part of movies, TV shows, and even video games. As a 2019 NPR article on the song's enduring success amusingly pointed out, it even appears in fictional weddings, being played at the wedding in the 1997 film *Soul Food*, starring Vanessa Williams, Vivica A. Fox, Michael Beach, and Mekhi Phifer.[1]

Over the years it's been in films as disparate as the 2006 Oscar nominee *Babel*, with the Japanese remix appearing in the film that stars Brad Pitt, Cate Blanchett, and others; the Steve Carell film *Dan in Real Life*; *Ted 2*, the sequel to the hit movie starring Mark Wahlberg and his talking stuffed bear; the 2019 horror film *Ma*; the 2019 film *Polar*; and the 2018 film *Traffik*.

On TV it's been on the hit shows *Mike & Molly*, *Shameless*, *9-1-1*, *Lethal Weapon*, *Better Things*, and *The Get Down*, among others. That list right there, which features comedy, drama, crime, and adventure, says so much of the song's versatility. Regardless of the subject matter, it is a song that just fits. People hear it, they recognize it, it takes them to a place. It has become an enduring anthem of the silver screen.

Proving that timelessness, in 2016, nearly forty years after it was first released, "September" made the soundtrack of two high-profile films, *The Nice Guys* with Russell Crowe and Ryan Gosling, and *Barbershop: The Next Cut*, starring Ice Cube, Cedric the Entertainer, and Regina Hall.

But there are probably two most iconic uses of "September" in cinema, both of which have contributed greatly to how the song has been handed down generationally, from grandparents to parents to kids.

The first is that the song is played in the final party scene before the end credits in the 2006 blockbuster *Night at the Museum*, starring Ben Stiller, Robin Williams, Carla Gugino, and Dick Van Dyke. In the scene, a smiling Stiller looks down from the second floor at the museum to see all of the historical exhibits that have come to life dancing and celebrating to "September."

If there was any lingering doubt that "September" is arguably the definitive song of celebration, this smash family film, which grossed $574 million worldwide, showed some of the most important characters in history, like Teddy Roosevelt (Williams) and Attila the Hun (played by Patrick Gallagher), partying to "September." So according to the film, this is the song that people would have been partying to throughout history.

The other seminal use in terms of the song's popularity came again in 2016, when alongside *The Nice Guys* and *Barbershop: The Next Cut*, EWF teamed with *Trolls* stars Justin Timberlake and Anna Kendrick to rerecord the song.

"What it did with the *Trolls* movie, it introduced us to a whole different generation of young kids," White says. "That's what it did. It's gone from generation to generation. But that lets you know the power of a song. If a song is really great it will go from generation to generation."

That has included covers as well, whether it was the 1999 remix by Phats & Small or gospel star Kirk Franklin covering it in 2007. White says he checks out the versions on occasion. And when he does it makes him smile.

Of the many different videos people have filmed around the world of themselves singing the song at celebrations, he says proudly, "There's been so many. As far as I'm concerned all of them are really good, some are singing different languages. You have different people doing it at parties, you have kids, that's the thing that I love. What I love is that it makes people happy."

For White that has been the greatest joy of the song, watching as it has been handed down generationally. And getting to hear directly from the fans their experiences with the song, whether it's getting married on September 21 or trying to give birth on that exact date.

"I just love the fact that people come up to me now and thank us for making songs like 'September,'" he says. "They thank us. That's what I get now. 'Thank you for making the music.'"

As one of the most joyous songs ever recorded, it has also become one of the absolute greatest closing songs in concert. You know the old showbiz adage, "Leave them wanting more"? Well, few things leave them wanting more more than "September."

For White, the most memorable performances of the song have involved closing down the night with everybody singing along, dancing and grooving to "September."

"I love when we did it at the Hollywood Bowl. We did it at the Hollywood Bowl a couple of times. And last year [2019] was really special," he says. "They both were because we did it at the Hollywood Bowl, September 21, which was declared EWF Day in Los Angeles.

"When we had Earth, Wind & Fire Day it was great. We got the keys to the city," White says.

However, the most iconic closing performance of the song was the one where the band got to be fans in the audience. In 2019, they were presented the Kennedy Center Honors and the night closed with John Legend, the Jonas Brothers, Ne-Yo, and Cynthia Erivo delivering a rendition so stellar that luminaries like Steven Spielberg and Sally Field are seen dancing in the crowd. And in the opening seconds of the song, husband and wife Tom Hanks and Rita Wilson turn and point to each other and sing, "Do you remember the twenty-first night of September?"

For White, being in the audience and watching everybody else get so much joy from the song, this was one of the most memorable performances of the song.

"They ended the Kennedy Center Honors with 'September,'" he says proudly. "It was just such a great song. You end a night in DC with something like that. And they were rocking, rocking, rocking."

Sure. As said, "September" is one of the great celebration anthems of all time. But it is so much more. Because it is a part of these historic events, big and small, from weddings to the World Cup to closing the Kennedy Center Honors, "September" becomes tied to people's memories, to their life stories. For any artist, that is the greatest compliment you can get.

White recalls his own days listening to the Beatles, Miles Davis, John Coltrane, and the music from *West Side Story*, or his own first dance at his wedding to McFadden & Whitehead's 1979 smash "Ain't No Stoppin' Us Now."

Now, with "September" he is part of creating a song that is an essential part of people's stories. "I think it's one of those songs that will resonate with people forever and it's just part of their, as we say, DNA," he says.

CHAPTER NINETEEN

CHIC

✦ "LE FREAK" ✦

*I*n the annals of American music there are arguably two companies that stand alone as the pinnacle of the record industry. One is Motown, known as the hit factory for its success with Smokey Robinson, Stevie Wonder, Four Tops, the Temptations, the Supremes, Marvin Gaye, and on and on.

The other is Atlantic Records, which, under the guidance of music legend Ahmet Ertegun until his death in 2006, has been home to some of the true all-time giants of music, from Aretha Franklin and Ray Charles to Led Zeppelin and Crosby, Stills & Nash. The list of artists who have graced the halls and studios of Atlantic Records is like a who's who of the Rock & Roll Hall of Fame.

So, CHIC mastermind Nile Rodgers is understandably proud when he points out that of all the hits to come in the more-than-seventy-year history of the iconic label, the biggest of those hits is a 1978 disco smash.

"The biggest record of my career is a CHIC record. It's 'Le Freak,' still the biggest-selling single in the history of Atlantic Records," Rodgers says. "So bigger than any Led Zeppelin record, Ray Charles, Bruno Mars, Aretha Franklin, anything. This silly little ditty that went, 'Ah, freak out.'"

To Rodgers, so much of the appeal of the song is that it captures the spirit and feel of the disco era it comes from. That was their way of covering up the fact the song was about a dance they didn't know how to do.

"It was supposed to teach you about a dance. And we didn't even know how to do the dance," Rodgers says. "So we just made up this cool song—we believed it to be cool—that talked about the environment and the people more than the dance 'cause we didn't know how to do the dance. But it was just this joyous-feeling thing."

For all of the song's joy, it was actually written in the heat of the moment after Rodgers and CHIC bandmate Bernard Edwards were denied entry to New York's famed Studio 54 on New Year's Eve 1977. They had been invited by Grace Jones, who'd forgotten to tell the staff to put them on the guest list.

Nine months later the song was released as a single and became an absolute monster, breaking records everywhere the song was available. It hit number one in Australia, Canada, New Zealand, and South Africa; number two in Belgium, France, the Netherlands, and Switzerland; and the top ten in Austria, Norway, Sweden, the UK, and West Germany.

But the song had its biggest impact in the States, becoming the first track ever at the time to hit the top spot on the Billboard Hot 100 three separate times (a record that would be unmatched for nearly thirty years, until 2008—when three songs, Leona Lewis's "Bleeding Love," T.I.'s "Whatever You Like," and T.I. and Rihanna's "Live Your Life"—achieved the feat). In addition to hitting number one on the Hot 100, it went to number one on both the R&B and dance club charts.

In short, you couldn't go anywhere from the fall of 1978 through much of 1979 without hearing revelers scream out in glee, "Ah, freak out." It's because of that infectious, easy-to-remember chant that Rodgers knew the band had a smash immediately.

"We were lucky in that our songs were anthems right away and that's what gave us a little bit of an edge when we played our concerts," he says. "Because we designed our music specifically for people to sing to. And we made our hooks so easy that you could sing it right away. Anybody could remember, 'Ah, freak out.' Even if you don't get the 'Le freak, c'est chic,' part you could just go, 'Freak out.'"

Hell, even when people got the lyrics wrong they still wanted to share in the enthusiasm and bliss of singing along to "Le Freak." Rodgers, who as a producer has worked with everyone from David Bowie and Madonna to Diana Ross and Duran Duran, recalls one of the most memorable nights of his life being spurred on in large part by "Le Freak."

"This is probably one of the most powerful nights of my life. So Nelson Mandela came to New York City and there was a big receiving line, a party at Robert DeNiro's restaurant. [Mandela] walked in, I was standing right behind Eddie Murphy because I had done the score to Coming to America, the first one. And [Mandela] walks in and he just lights up like a Christmas tree. He says, 'Eddie,' and he's happy because Coming to America was this cultural phenomenon that he said resonated across the entire continent of Africa," Rodgers recalls. "But then somebody told him that I was the guy who wrote 'We Are Family' and I wrote a song called 'Africa' ('Le Freak'). Many French-speaking African countries—as you well know the French colonized a lot of Africa—thought we were singing, 'A-frica!' That's what they thought we were saying because the chorus that sings 'Le Freak' is Luther Vandross, Bernard Edwards, myself, Alfa Anderson, Diva Gray, all these people from diverse backgrounds and cultures that none of us speak French. And so to Africans it was a cool way of saying, 'Africa.' Nelson Mandela was standing there and all his friends were going, 'Yes, he's the guy who wrote "Africa."'"

So did Rodgers ever tell Mandela the song was called "Le Freak"? "Of course I didn't correct him. No way, you do not correct Nelson Mandela," Rodgers says, laughing. "Because he was also going on and on about 'We Are Family' actually, which, in a strange way meant more to him because when he was in prison, he said the white prison guards would have those little transistor radios and he would hear it coming from the radios and he could tell from the sounds of the women's voices that they were Black. And he said a song by Black girls sung by the white prison guards talking about how they were going to be a family, he knew at that point South Africa would not be under apartheid forever. So that's really what we were talking about. But somebody then said to him, 'But he also wrote "Africa."'"

For Rodgers, one of the preeminent hitmakers of the last five decades, it is not surprising that discussion of one of his hits would lead to another. A conversation with him winds from Diana Ross's "I'm Coming Out" and Madonna's "Like a Virgin" to the B-52's "Love Shack" and Daft Punk's "Get Lucky." But his work with CHIC holds a special place in his heart.

So having a "silly" little disco song recognized by one of the great world figures of the twentieth century is a significant honor. Of course, the secret that Rodgers's fans and peers recognize is that there is nothing simple about "Le Freak."

Sure, the infectious hook and beat of the song invite fans to sing, dance, and skate along with abandon. But musicians recognize underneath that joyful beat is the musical adventure and sophistication that have garnered Rodgers seven Grammy nominations and three awards.

As he recalls, the song's advanced interlude blew away fellow producer Mark Ronson (known for his work with Amy Winehouse, Bruno Mars, and Adele, among others).

"I remember Mark Ronson saying to me that he couldn't believe it. When he went and bought the song as a kid—Mark is very sophisticated—so he said he was waiting for the middle eight and he says, 'Holy cow, it's not a middle eight, it's not even a middle sixteen, it's a damn middle thirty-two! There's no such thing as a middle thirty-two in a pop song,'" Rodgers says. "And we just start playing. So it was an expression about those times, those freewheeling, open-minded times."

For Ronson, the song had the same mind-expanding affect Rodgers felt when he walked into a New York disco with his then girlfriend and heard Donna Summer's "Love to Love You Baby," Village People's "San Francisco," and Eddie Kendricks's "Girl You Need a Change of Mind" back to back to back.

It was right then, as he recalls, that the template for CHIC's "Le Freak" was born. "Our music lived for the breakdown," he says. "That's what I heard on Donna Summer that night. That's what I heard on Eddie Kendricks that night, that's what I heard on the Village People that night. I was like, 'Wow.'"

Watch a crowd today as Rodgers plays "Le Freak" or the band's other number one hit of that summer of '79, "Good Times," and it's as if one is transported back in time to when disco ruled the world.

He got to experience that feeling while appearing at the legendary Glastonbury Festival in southwest England in 2013, one of several times in recent years he has been a star on the bill.

"The first time we played Glastonbury our capacity was only supposed to be thirty-five thousand or something like that," he says. "And [the CEO of Glastonbury] told me Glastonbury had only been shut down once before the night we played. So the night we played was the second time they closed down the event because so many people charged our stage that we had almost double the capacity. This was also when 'Get Lucky' had just come out and it was complete pandemonium. When we went into 'Good Times,' holy cow, you'd never seen anything like it. I said to the CEO I honestly felt I could step off the stage and the vibe was so strong that it would actually hold me up. I felt like a force field of good vibes."

Good vibes and good times are what CHIC, "Le Freak," and disco were and are all about to Rodgers. Reflecting on the song's lofty status in the pantheon of Atlantic's storied history, he says, "To this day nobody has surpassed those sales. And that says a lot to me because it's just a song that makes people feel happy."

The song's lasting legacy also has a special place for him and his disco brethren from that time. Rodgers, like so many of his peers, wasn't spared from the disco backlash that came in the early eighties. As he recalls, nobody wanted to work with them. "It was like we had a scarlet disco across our chest."

Forty-two years later the song has been a major part of popular culture, appearing in films such as *Shrek 2*, *Mystery Men*, *Toy Story 3*, *Diary of a Wimpy Kid*, and many more. Through all these films the song has continued to take on new life, making that refrain of "Ah, freak out" one that fans of all ages, from five to eighty, can still shout with joy.

For Rodgers, it is one of the great achievements in his Rock & Roll Hall of Fame career. Speaking about the feeling of watching fans sing along, he says emotionally, "Honestly, it's one of the greatest honors ever. Every time we play a show I feel like that."

Speaking of honors, that silly little disco song that fans tried to forget because of the "disco sucks" backlash was named the twenty-first biggest song of the first fifty-five years of the Billboard Hot 100. And much more significantly in 2018, it was selected by the Library of Congress for preservation in the National Recording Registry for being "culturally, artistically, or historically significant."[1]

Rodgers says he isn't the type to be vindictive, but after all the antidisco backlash, to have "Le Freak" stand the test of time for both fans and critics, yeah, it's unquestionably satisfying. And without question, another forty years from now, fans will still be screaming "Ah, freak out" every time the song comes on in a club, a movie, anywhere. Just try not to sing along. I'll bet you can't.

CHAPTER TWENTY

TOTO

✦ "AFRICA" ✦

OTO's "Africa" was once playfully selected as the "Best Song Ever," according to science. It was back in 2017, when Gizmodo asked neuroscientists and music fans what makes a great song. After examining all the elements of a great song, and succumbing to social media pressure from fans who voted for "Africa," a New York University psychology researcher declared "Africa" the winner.[1]

Even TOTO's David Paich, who came up with the original idea and lyrics for the song before bringing it to the rest of the band, laughs at that idea. "Someone asked me about that and they caught me off guard. I didn't mean to be rude or anything. But an interviewer caught me off guard, a guy said, 'This is the greatest song—they've proven it scientifically. It's the greatest song ever written,'" Paich says. "I said, 'Is that guy a comedian or something? Who on earth would say that?' I was stunned when I hear things like that."

When Paich shares the initial story behind the song, his skepticism of science's heady accolade is understandable. Though he recalls writing it and having a good feeling. "I do remember writing it. The very first time I heard the chorus which was in my studio in Sherman Oaks. I was on the piano playing and all of a sudden I realized I struck gold," he says.

But his own band didn't agree he says, laughing. "This was going to be an extra cut on the *TOTO IV* album. And when I played it originally for the guys, I played the little verse I think," he recalls. "And everybody said, 'Hey, that's gonna be great on your solo album.' Which means it's not going to go on *TOTO IV*, basically that's what they're saying."

Thankfully for Paich and the millions of fans who have loved the song since its release forty years ago, the band reconsidered shelving Paich's idea. "We had some extra time left over in the studio. And so the guys said, 'Well, hey, let's mess around with that last song and it can be the last song on the record,'" he says. "Because we thought we already had the singles and stuff covered with 'Rosanna.' And we thought 'Make Believe' was going to be a big hit, but it wasn't."

Though the band wasn't immediately enthused about the song, nor did they expect it to be a hit, Paich does remember the recording session, with the legendary Al Schmitt (who'd worked with Frank Sinatra, Bob Dylan, Brian Wilson, Paul McCartney, and more) as being memorable.

"It was a very special record to make. Because we got to actually kind of record the way the Beatles used to record and stuff, which was to make some loops," he says. "We made a loop of percussionists Jeff [Porcaro] and Lenny Castro. And on analog tape, which is two-inch tape, which people don't even use the stuff anymore. And we wrapped it around, cause we had Al Schmitt, the famous engineer, who I've known since I was ten

years old because he used to work with my father on jazz records. We had Al, who's done everything in the studio imagin-
able. He cut the tape, after we picked the two bars that we wanted.
He spliced the tape and we put up mic stands. So it was actually
going over, almost like a Lionel train set. This splice around the
room, around these mic stands. It's really entertaining to understand the mechanics of it. So the first track that was laid down
was Jeff Porcaro and Lenny Castro. And then one at a time we
started putting parts on it. I put a guide keyboard part on there.
And then David Hungate put his bass on. [Steve] Lukather put
his great guitar stuff on. And we started getting vocals on there."

These days the song has been labeled a soft rock classic. And
the African beats Paich and his bandmates put on there are labeled world music. But to them, it was simply finding the sounds
and style that worked for them. "World music they call it now.
But we were just experimenting the way we like to do," he says.
"That's one of the fun things about TOTO."

So after the inspired recording session, did the band understand that the song they had just cut would go on to be their only
number one song on the Billboard Hot 100 ever?

"We had no idea it was going to be a hit record. On the con-
trary, we thought that was the least it was going to be. We
thought, *Okay, here's an album cut, just a footnote after the album
is really over*," he says. "So we were very pleasantly surprised; well
most everybody."

For Paich, as the vocalist on the band's biggest hit, the song
brought its own set of pressure and expectations. "It's funny, I
always get to sing live a couple of token songs on the record
that usually aren't the hits and stuff like this. But this one became a hit so it was up to me to perform it every night live," he
says. "So it was challenging; it's been a very gratifying journey
with that song."

The song has become a favorite live, often closing out the set, Paich points out. But just as the song didn't connect immediately with the band, it was an inauspicious live start.

"I can't recall the first time I played it live because we've played it so many times and they all kind of meld into one. I know I was pretty nervous at the time because I hadn't played it and sung it before live. And it's a lot of words going with a lot of keyboard playing and stuff like that," he says. "It's like walking and chewing gum at the same time but a bit more difficult than that."

It did take off fairly quickly though with fans once he mastered the song. "We were performing it live as an encore in a lot of places. Because it was such a crowd-pleaser as well. So there was a lot of factors involved with that. What's great about playing for an audience is you get an immediate response. You can tell if they love it or they're just lukewarm about it, or if they don't like it you'll see everybody leaving to go get a beer or something," he says, laughing. "It's that easy."

Now, forty years later, every performance of the song is a celebration of the band and the fans' storied history with the song. "I always look forward to playing it live onstage. It's a very fun tune to play, it's a challenging song to play. But we get into a long jam on the end where there's some crowd participation and some solos. We really open it up," he says. "It's very tribal and very organic. Has a lot of humanity in it for me."

Upon release the song was an instant hit. But funnily enough its initial success wasn't in the pop or rock world, again surprising Paich. "The president of Columbia, which is Sony Music now, called me and says, 'We're getting a lot of action from the dance charts.' And I said, 'Well what song?' And he said, 'Africa.' And I was just bowled over," Paich recalls. "I said, 'Really?' He said, 'Yeah, it's been on a playlist in the New York discos.' And I said, 'Really, that's incredible.' But now when I think about it, it makes perfect sense because Jeff's hypnotic drumbeat has four on the floor which is iconic to dance records. We never intended it to be like that, but I certainly enjoyed the fact that it was a dance record because we like people to sing and dance to our music."

The evolution of "Africa," like all the songs in this anthology, from a chart-topping smash to an anthem for the ages was a gradual one. And it started with the song being used in seemingly every movie and TV show in the last forty years.

"Cable was playing and I started getting a lot of requests from my publisher that this show wanted it, and this show wanted it, and this show wanted it. There were a lot of Adam Sandler requests. Then got one from *Stranger Things*. And we noticed that it was getting substantial play on cable," he says. "And then in 2010, when we went back on the road to help Mike Porcaro out with his ailment, we started really picking up there when streaming came around and so that's when I could tell the amount of requests that it had, TV and movies, different things like that. That it was gaining momentum."

Because of the song's instantly recognizable opening and how synonymous "Africa" is with the early eighties, it is a song that can be used in media for both nostalgia and entertainment. Paich has particularly enjoyed when "Africa" has been used for humor, which has been often.

"Some people have done tongue-in-cheek, little humorous things with it. I think when Jimmy Fallon and Justin Timberlake were on Jimmy Fallon's show. And they were Boy Scouts back in the eighties. And they were in a tent and they started singing 'Africa,'" he remembers. "I got the request for 'Africa' and I thought, *The band's going to play them on and off*. That's a normal request for a TV show. But they put it into a script, an act, where these boys were staying up past curfew and they were singing

'Africa' in the tent. And they kept singing it, getting reprimanded by the camp counselor and everything, and they kept singing it and singing it and singing it over and over again and I was just sitting amazed going, 'Is anybody seeing this?' We all called each other, we were all excited like kids, and we all called each other, like, 'Jimmy Fallon and Justin Timberlake are doing the song.' Sometimes you get honored in a comedic fashion, it can be just as honoring as playing the Royal Albert Hall. There's different kinds of satisfaction and it's all satisfying."

Many of his favorite uses of the song were tongue in cheek, whether on *South Park*, *The Goldbergs*, *Scrubs*, *American Dad*, or *Family Guy*. "*Family Guy*, where he gets married. He goes to his bachelor party and he goes and gets a lap dance from his wife and that's how they met. And they're playing 'Africa' while he's getting a lap dance. On *Family Guy*, everyone loves that show too."

The consistent use in popular culture, especially in the succession of hit animated series, has been a big factor in introducing the song to new generations of fans. And if it weren't for that, the online petition by a fan to get Weezer to cover the song might never have happened. But Paich gratefully acknowledges and appreciates the role Weezer played in bringing the song to a new generation of fans.

"It definitely had an impact with millennials and kids that are just younger. My nephew, who is one of our road managers, said, 'What famous band recorded the song "Africa" back in the eighties?' It was on a crossword puzzle. And my nephew wrote 'Weezer' and sent it me. It was funny," he says. "But I dug Weezer's version of it because it respected the original version. They made it their own when it came to the solo and stuff like that. But, in general, they followed our blueprint and they did a pretty good job I think. My daughter, who was teaching Chinese at the time; she speaks Chinese. Her friend in Beijing called her.

[Weezer] had also done 'Rosanna,' a version of it. And when 'Africa' came out we first got a call from Beijing, '"Africa" is doing really big over here with Weezer. You guys should turn it on.' I wasn't even hip to Weezer doing any of our stuff. And it was just very exciting."

Between the Weezer version and the TV and film uses, the song has become a favorite of fans of all ages, something that never fails to please or impress Paich. "But I get this a lot of times. A lot of people, neighbors and friends, will come up and say their twelve-year-old girl loves your song 'Africa.' And I'll say, 'Sing a little bit of it.' And a little twelve-year-old girl will sing the chorus to 'Africa' for me. And it just touches my heart. It just means we've transcended a lot of issues in the world and we're still connecting to a certain audience. And Weezer just solidified that concept."

Any song that endures for decades goes through a roller coaster of ups and downs to reach its status as a permanent part of pop culture. But few have gone through the Mr. Toad's Wild Ride "Africa" has, from a throwaway album cut the band didn't even want to record initially to one of the most popular songs of all time.

"It's had an amazing journey. It has legs of its own. Literally it sprung legs of its own. I'm just amazed by it all," Paich says. "Like I said, 'Africa' was what they used to call a sleeper on the charts. Which is a tune that becomes a hit that you never expected to become a hit."

But it has become so much more than a hit. Yes, it hit number one. Many songs have done that though. "Africa" has become a part of people's lives and consciousness. The song has become to them what Elton John and the Beatles were to Paich.

"It's between a Beatles song and an Elton John song. 'Levon,' by Elton John. I think that's an innovative masterpiece. And the

Beatles, it's just like every song they did," he says of his favorite songs. "Lukather just did a track that Joseph Williams and I wrote for his album. And Ringo played drums on it. And talk about a pinch-me moment. There's a film of the playing. And he's playing drums on one of my songs, the song that I cowrote with Joseph and Luke. And the Beatles, I think *Sgt. Pepper's* could be the greatest album ever made. Especially for the time it came out. And it still stands the test of time for me."

So crazy, that those feelings he had listening to *Sgt. Pepper's Lonley Hearts Club Band* and "Levon" he hears from fans about TOTO and "Africa." "I am so grateful for the people that write these letters and make these comments about it. They're so passionate about the music when they hear it and the things that they write just touches one's heart," he says. "It has touched so many people and I get so many letters and comments from people around the world. From Africa, from South Africa. And it's been really a blessing to us. It's been very soul-satisfying and very healing to have been able to have been involved with that song."

He still gets to enjoy that blessing and to feel the impact the song and his music with TOTO has made on people in regular interactions with fans. He has had some very special moments with fans.

"A couple, several, said they had named their new baby Rosanna after your song. A newborn baby. So that's pretty eye-opening right there," he says. "And some people would get tattoos of the continent of Africa on their shoulder. With the TOTO sword and everything. But the ones where people would name their newborn child Rosanna after the song, that just blew my mind."

CHAPTER TWENTY-ONE

LINDA RONSTADT

✦ "SKYLARK" ✦

ike 99 percent of artists, Linda Ronstadt is a perfectionist. Throughout her entire iconic career, which saw her get elected to the Rock & Roll Hall of Fame on her first ballot in 2014, she says there are only a handful of her vocal performances that measure up to her high standards.

For instance, she will not listen to her version of the Eagles' "Desperado," though Don Henley said her 1973 version of the hit helped bring the song to the mainstream and he called her version "beautiful and poignant."

But she says of it, "I can't stand my recording of it. I was so intimidated by Don's vocal on his version of it that I wouldn't record it. But then I liked the song so much that I had to record it anyway."

Ronstadt has had a number of hugely successful and influential songs—"You're No Good," "Blue Bayou," "When Will I Be Loved," "It's So Easy," "Hurt So Bad," "Heat Wave," "Just One Look"—but as I said, few stand out to her, which, having talked to thousands of artists, is not unusual.

In her estimation, though, despite all those hits, she didn't really become a vocalist until 1980. "I learned to sing better. I didn't know what I was doing when I started. I hadn't a clue at shows," she says. "The more I sang, the better musicians I worked with, the better I learned. I was a slow learner; it took me a long time to learn how to sing."

But when she did, the results were spectacular, even in her very critical eyes. So when she finds a performance she does like, you know that song is incredibly special and has gone through the most rigorous of inspections to pass the Ronstadt ear test.

Her version of "Skylark," penned in 1941 by Hoagy Carmichael and Johnny Mercer, featured on her 1984 smash album, *Lush Life*, a record that earned her a Grammy nomination and became her tenth platinum album at the time, is one of those handful of songs—along with her work with Dolly Parton and Emmylou Harris on the *Trio* record, and the Mexican song "Mi Ranchito"—that Ronstadt looks back fondly on.

For starters, she loved the experience of working with the legendary composer/band leader/arranger Nelson Riddle, with whom she teamed for a trio of albums from 1983 to 1986 (Riddle passed in 1985 during the making of the last of the trilogy, *For Sentimental Reasons*).

"I liked working with Nelson Riddle. He's a genius," she says. "I'd been listening to his records for years. I was a fan of the [Frank] Sinatra records that he made. Also he made records with Ella Fitzgerald and Rosemary Clooney. Really good. I always tried to work with the best players I could. Nelson was one of the highlights of that experience."

As mentioned, "Skylark" appeared on *Lush Life*, which was the second album with Riddle, following 1983's unexpected blockbuster, *What's New*, which spent eighty-one weeks on the Billboard album chart and hit number three for five weeks, trailing only Michael Jackson's *Thriller* and Lionel Richie's *Can't Slow Down* during those five weeks. Looking back, an album of standard songs at that time rivaling Jackson and Richie on the charts during the early rise of MTV—when upbeat new wave and pop songs, such as Jackson's "Billie Jean," Men at Work's "Down Under," The Eurythmics' "Sweet Dreams (Are Made of This)," and Irene Cara's "Flashdance . . . What a Feeling" dominated the charts—is now virtually impossible to imagine.

But the combination of rock star Ronstadt and bandleader Riddle proved to be a massive hit. For Ronstadt, commercial appeal was never factored into the equation though. She admits that the idea of the three albums was just for her, as a fan of these classic songs. "I didn't think about that before I recorded it. At all. It occurred to me afterward. I only did it because I liked the songs. It was for purely selfish reasons," she says. "I'm delighted that it sold but that wasn't why I did it and it wouldn't matter if it hadn't sold."

As big as *What's New* was, *Lush Life* and "Skylark," in particular, stand out because, to her, on her second album with Riddle, her singing in the world of standard songs had improved greatly. "I knew how to sing that music better because it was the second album I made," she says. "I'd been on the road with material already for a year and I knew how to sing it better."

For a perfectionist like Ronstadt, her appreciation for her rendition of "Skylark" came down to having time to learn the song and becoming more comfortable with singing it on a regular basis.

"I had more rehearsal time with it, rehearsal at the piano," she says. "And there wasn't so much change in the orchestra. An orchestration like Nelson likes is a whole other journey. Some things are written more in strict time signature, some are in legato, and some are in rubato. It's hard to know what it's going to be."

Talk to Ronstadt and it is clear how seriously she takes her craft of singing. It's so easy to see why she became one of the most acclaimed and beloved vocalists of her time. To her, singing is an art form to be taken seriously. That includes practice. And that, for her, is the biggest difference between the songs, like "Skylark," on *Lush Life*, her second album with Riddle, and those like, for example, "Someone to Watch Over Me" on *What's New*.

Talking about "Someone to Watch Over Me," her biggest issue with her performance was not having the time to properly integrate herself into the song's nuances and layers.

"It was one of my first picks but then I tried to sing it and I realized how difficult it was to sing. It's hard to sing, if you don't know what you're doing phrasing wise. And I didn't know the song well enough when I recorded it," she says. "Because we couldn't afford to rehearse with the orchestra. It was too expensive. And you only get a couple times through; you only get three passes through with the orchestra so it was the first time I ever sang a song in that key, with the orchestra. So I learned to sing it onstage."

Even now, after her version of the song became a hit and the album a massive success, she won't listen to her version of "Someone to Watch Over Me." "No, I can't bear to listen to it. It's just so incorrectly phrased. I learned to get the phrasing better when I sang," she says. "Any song, hours and weeks of learning it, and refining it, just exploring it. I didn't have the luxury with any of those songs. *What's New* was the first take that we did, the first time I ever sang that song in my key. And just myself singing it, and practice with the orchestra. We did two more takes and we chose the first one."

Thankfully, for her, she is able to go back and listen to some of the other great versions of the song, including Ella Fitzgerald's version, which is the first one she remembers hearing.

"I thought she sang it right, she sang the melody, she sang the words, she really addressed the feeling I thought," she says. "Another thing, it's a beautifully written song. If it were a sailboat it would have exquisite rigging. You climb around the rigging and see what it's made of and how it's constructed. It's a wonderful thing. The Gershwin Brothers knew what they were doing. Both musically and lyrically, it's a perfect fit."

She ranks it as one of the top two pop songs ever written. "For me it's tied with 'Somewhere Over the Rainbow' as the greatest pop song ever written. They're both songs about yearning, and 'Someone to Watch Over Me' was a little bit more hopeful than 'Somewhere Over the Rainbow,'" she says. "'Somewhere Over the Rainbow' starts off with hope and then you fantasize about what it would be like, happiness and whatever, that freedom they're yearning for and then started realizing that it's never going to happen but hoping anyway. 'Someone to Watch Over Me' is just pure hope and longing."

One of the joys of talking to Ronstadt about this era is her love and knowledge of these songs, like when she discusses "Skylark." She knew she loved the song. As she said, the impetus for the trilogy of standards albums with Riddle was her fandom of these songs, which she had grown up with, including, of course, "Skylark." Although the song has been recorded by everyone from Bing Crosby, Bobby Darin, and Bob Dylan to Aretha Franklin, Rosemary Clooney, and Ella Fitzgerald, there isn't one version Ronstadt heard first that shaped her view of the song. Rather, it's been part of the fabric of her life.

"I've just always heard it. It's always been there in the literature. I can't think of anybody's vocal I listened to," she says. "It's like in a piano bar. If you go into a piano bar, I always ask for 'Skylark.' It has nice changes, a beautiful melody, and nice sentiment to the lyrics. So I have my own way of singing it."

In her way of singing it she tapped into the longing of the song, which Mercer wrote about his affair with Judy Garland. Legend has it that Mercer wrestled with the song for a year before finally finding the voice he was seeking in the song. To Ronstadt there is no question he finally got it right.

"It's a terrible yearning. It's knowing there's something just a little bit better right around the corner. And you've never felt that before and you really want to have it," she says. "Not necessarily love; it's just a way of living, a way of being, a way of being in a state of grace. It's just yearning."

That Ronstadt would appreciate the level of vulnerability and openness Mercer captured in the lyrics for "Skylark" doesn't surprise her. She calls herself a fan of his lyric writing for sure.

"I appreciated the fineness of the writing. I always do. I always thought it was a well-written song and then when I sang it I realized how well written it was," she says. "Johnny Mercer was a brilliant composer. He could sing too. So his songs were written very nicely for singers."

As a lifelong fan of "Skylark," Ronstadt had an idea she could give the song the voice she felt it deserved. But she admits she didn't know how successful her rendition would be.

"I always knew that I could ride it and soar. I always thought it was a good song, that I could sing it," she says. "But I didn't know that it could be a real vehicle for me. Regardless of what everybody else thinks, I felt, I was just thinking that I owned it. It was taking me where I wanted to go."

So now when she listens back to her version, what does she hear? What does the story she conveys tell her? "Longing. And fairly full execution that he'll achieve it," she says.

AEROSMITH
© Norman Seeff

BARRY MANILOW
Bobby Bank/WireImage via Getty Images

BOB MARLEY
© *Neal Preston*

BRAD DELSON OF LINKIN PARK

Photo by Scott Uchida/Courtesy Linkin Park

CARLY SIMON

© Ken Regan

CHIC

Courtesy of Nile Rodgers Productions

CROSBY, STILLS, NASH & YOUNG

© Henry Diltz

DON McLEAN

© Barry Schultz

EARTH, WIND & FIRE

© Richard E. Aaron Estate

THE 5TH DIMENSION

Michael Ochs Archives/Michael Ochs Archives via Getty Images

FLEETWOOD MAC

© *Neal Preston*

HALL & OATES
© *Timothy White*

JANIS IAN
© *Barry Schultz*

JEFFERSON AIRPLANE
© *Herb Greene*

KISS
© Bob Gruen

LINDA RONSTADT
© *Henry Diltz*

MY CHEMICAL ROMANCE AT AVALON
Jeff Kravitz/FilmMagic via Getty Images

NEIL DIAMOND
© *Richard E. Aaron Estate*

SHANIA TWAIN
Courtesy of Shania Twain

TEARS FOR FEARS

Gie Knaeps/Hulton Archive via Getty Images

AL JARDINE AND BRIAN WILSON OF THE BEACH BOYS

Courtesy of Brian Wilson

THE DOORS
© Gloria Stavers

THE JACKSON 5
© John R. Hamilton

THE SPINNERS
© *Richard E. Aaron Estate*

THE TEMPTATIONS
Michael Ochs Archives/Michael Ochs Archives via Getty Images

TLC
© *Timothy White*

TOM WAITS, SANTA ROSA, 2002
© *Anton Corbijn*

DAVID PAICH OF TOTO
© Kevin Albinder

U2, SANTA CRUZ DE TENERIFE, 1991
© Anton Corbijn

CHAPTER TWENTY-TWO

TEARS
FOR FEARS

✦ "EVERYBODY WANTS TO ✦
RULE THE WORLD"

*L*ike the vast majority of artists, Tears for Fears' Roland Orzabal doesn't go back and listen to his own music. So when he does stumble upon the band's 1985 chart-topping smash, "Everybody Wants to Rule the World," in public, he listens to it almost from the standpoint of a fan.

"I hear it every now and again. I'm in a supermarket and it comes on and even now, it sounds so fresh and—what's the word?—almost modest," he says. "There's nothing macho about it. It's very understated in a way. And very, very simple. I think it's got those magic progressions. I remember as a kid, 'I'd Like to Teach the World to Sing (In Perfect Harmony),' by the New Seekers. Someone told me it's the simplicity of the melody. It's just that simple melodic climb."

From the moment those opening chimes, which make you think of Christmas, kick in, Tears for Fears take listeners on a jangly journey of pure pop perfection. It is a masterpiece of sing-song joviality, as engaging and joyful a melody as, for example, Electric Light Orchestra's "Mr. Blue Sky," which was named the happiest song of all time in a British poll.

If you've ever seen Tears for Fears in concert you know it is physically impossible to not break into song and dance with an ear-to-ear grin when the fluorescent aural light of "Everybody Wants to Rule the World" shines across the night sky.

Hard to believe it started as a song called "Everybody Wants to Go to War," which morphed into a general attack on those who are power hungry.

"It was originally called 'Everybody Wants to Go to War.' It was written, again, in the height of the Cold War between Russia and the United States. So that was always in the back of my mind," Orzabal says. "But it's a little bit to do with power struggles. There were a lot of power struggles going on with the record company. So it's not just militaristic. It's also personal about people who have ambition. There's the line, 'So sad they had to fade it.' Which kind of sounds like, 'What the hell does that mean?' It's a reference to the fact that we had a big argument with the record company about the length of 'Shout.' Because it was eight minutes and they were saying, they're not going to play it on the radio because it's too long. So we had an argument about that and in the end they trimmed five seconds off the fade. So, for instance I use that, a reference to fading 'Shout' for five seconds."

With "Everybody Wants to Rule the World," Tears for Fears hit upon one of the most successful tools in pop music for captivating audiences: the juxtaposition of an upbeat, happy melody with dark subject matter.

Think about the Beatles' "Help!" The frenzied pace of the song gives it an almost playful feel musically. It's a song six-year-olds can scream and shake along to. Then you look at the lyrics. It's a plea for help masked in pop playfulness, a trick Tears for Fears captured in their own way masterfully on "Everybody Wants to Rule the World," mixing sociopolitical commentary with pop bliss.

For Orzabal, that mix of pop hooks and thoughtful, provocative subject matter remains a big part of the appeal of Tears for Fears, who continue to be a thriving recording and touring band thirty-seven years after the release of the song.

"I think one thing we managed to do successfully was create pop music but with darker lyrics. In fact we managed to avoid writing a pure love song," he says proudly. "I think 'Head Over Heels' was a bit of an anomaly for us. But 'Pale Shelter,' that's not really a love song. It's a love song to your parents, a song about rejection. 'Mad World' is up-tempo, it's upbeat, it's kind of uplifting. But it's pretty terrifying lyrics: 'The dreams in which I'm dying are the best I've ever had.' And I think that 'Everybody Wants to Rule the World' is similar. Again it's political."

"Everybody Wants to Rule the World" was an immediate global smash, hitting number one in Canada and New Zealand and the Billboard Hot 100 in the US, as well as number two in Ireland, the Netherlands, and the UK. The song ended up as the seventh-biggest song of 1985 on the year-end Billboard Hot 100 charts.

Despite the jangly hook, a song so overtly political might seem a surprising choice to become such a massive global pop anthem. However, that era of music, the mid-eighties, when "Everybody Wants to Rule the World" did indeed rule the world, was a particularly prolific and fruitful one for socially conscious artists.

During that same mid-eighties period, U2 had hit singles with "Sunday Bloody Sunday," about the conflict in Ireland, and

"Pride (In the Name of Love)," a tribute to Martin Luther King Jr. R.E.M., Peter Gabriel, and Sting also were scoring chart success with social anthems.

Perhaps most similarly to "Everybody Wants to Rule the World," the title track to Bruce Springsteen's blockbuster *Born in the U.S.A.* album became a global hit, though its criticism of American policy and the way Vietnam veterans were treated was soundly misunderstood and co-opted by then president Ronald Reagan, who famously referenced Springsteen at a campaign stop in New Jersey on September 19, 1984, during the height of the popularity of *Born in the U.S.A.*

Though "Everybody Wants to Rule the World" was never name-checked by a global political leader on that scale, Orzabal admits he has seen some pretty interesting interpretations of the song.

To him, the song's lyrics and message became much clearer when New Zealand superstar Lorde covered the song for the soundtrack to the film *The Hunger Games: Catching Fire.*

"In many ways, the way that she has done it is probably more respectful to the lyrics," Orzabal says of her interpretation. "That's the thing that stands out with the Lorde version. You are confronted with the lyrics far more; they don't just fly by you. You can't ignore them."

The band is such a fan of her version they have incorporated it into their own live show the last few years. "We started using that as our intro tape, live. So we would walk on to that song," he says. "So we would play that live, walk on to it, and then immediately start our version. Which in and of itself is crazy but it worked really, really well."

In a way, Lorde's version got to fulfill every artist's fantasy for Orzabal. Every artist is a perfectionist who wishes they could go back and redo things in their songs, no matter how successful.

Lorde emphasizing the lyrics allowed Orzabal to make that change vicariously. Because, as he explains, the way the song was done was a result of the writing and the group dynamic, not his decision alone.

He admits he didn't even like the song when he first started writing it. "The thing that held me back—which often happens with lyrics—you've got this, 'Everybody Wants to Go to War.' It was rubbish, in my opinion," he says.

However, when you hear him tell of that pressure that originally came with writing the song, his initial frustration with it isn't so surprising.

"I was given a month off to write songs for the second Tears for Fears album," he recalls. "We'd been struggling since *The Hurting* and the record company were extremely desperate for another single, another single. It was almost like whatever song we came up with was going to be the next single. So we released 'The Way You Are.' It didn't do that well. And then we had another song, just one more song called 'Mothers Talk,' and yes, we were struggling. So everyone said, 'Roland, go away for a month, no, don't go away for a month. Go home for a month and come up with some new songs.'"

He has his late wife, Caroline, who tragically passed in 2017, to thank in large part for not giving up on the "rubbish" song. "It was actually my late wife who liked the song as well," he explains. "So I thought, *Well, why does she like it?*"

She wasn't the only one. Producer Chris Hughes was equally enamored with what Orzabal had thus far. "I played this to Chris and he was absolutely obsessed with it," he says. "So Chris really sort of forced us to do it."

Reflecting on the song's origins, Orzabal says Talking Heads were a huge inspiration. "I took a LinnDrum machine, and I had my acoustic guitar and I had a Prophet-5 synthesizer. But what I was doing, at the time we were always trying to imitate our idols. Talking Heads and especially the *Remain in Light* album," he says. "So I would program some more esoteric stuff into the LinnDrum but there was one beat that sort of fascinated me which was the 'shuffle beat,' as Chris used to call it, of 'Everybody Wants to Rule the World.' And there was also a high-hat pattern, from a track called 'Throw Away the Key' by an eighties duo called Linx and that was the offbeat ts-ts-ts. So I put that in the drum machine. And I D-tuned the acoustic guitar to a bottom D. And came up with the main verse riffs. So all I had was the verse, [sings] 'Welcome to your life' and the bridge, 'da-da-da-da-da-da . . . everybody wants to go to war.' That's all I had."

He goes on to talk about how the song expanded. "So we were recording the body of songs. And then at the end of the day, I would get on guitar, Ian Stanley would get on keyboards, Chris would get on synth bass. We'd have the LinnDrum pattern that I'd programmed at home. And we would just improvise," he says. "And that's when I came up with the guitar figure, the intro. And then it took on a life of its own. Ian came up with the chords for the middle eight. And Chris as well, so at that point the song pretty much had its structure. But it wasn't really until we started recording it with all the fills and all that kind of stuff. And the feel. Every time we put the reels up, it was like a shock."

It was out of that group effort that the song went from rubbish to what would eventually become a worldwide smash. "It was like a pleasant surprise. It was almost like opening the door and walking out of the kitchen and there's a beautiful summer's day," he says. "It was very, very unlike anything we were doing on *Songs from the Big Chair*. Which a lot of it is very intense. And then you've got this crazy, fresh air, summer's day track. But we still didn't know. You never really know until it's really finished, how it would turn out."

How it would turn out is it became an instant hit, which Orzabal saw by the time the band came to America to tour for *Songs from the Big Chair*. "Our first show in America, ever, was in Hartford, Connecticut. And we were already number one with 'Everybody Wants to Rule the World.' So yes, I would say there was an instant connection because it was so popular already," he says. "But it's more; I think nowadays you start to see the impact because it's been around for decades. It's really when we kick into that song live that you get to see the effect it's had on the audience. More, I think, than in the beginning."

That is, in part, because of the song's continual use in popular culture. In a true testament to the way Tears for Fears mixed the serious subject matter with the pop hooks, the song has been used in HBO's groundbreaking *The Wire* and in the Mira Sorvino and Lisa Kudrow comedy *Romy and Michele's High School Reunion*. Not many songs could fit both those projects. It's also been in *Psych*, the Netflix hit *To All The Boys I've Loved Before*, the Adam Sandler film *Click*, and so much more.

One of the more surprising uses to some might be in the hit N.W.A. biopic *Straight Outta Compton*. Until you remember that the film takes place in the eighties, and as Orzabal points out, the second their version of "Everybody Wants to Rule the World" comes in, it is like time travel.

"Obviously, without question, our version of the song is instant nostalgia," he says. "If someone's programming music for a film or an ad, and they want to pop everyone straight back to that year, that's one of the ways of doing it."

But, for his personal choice, he now actually prefers the Lorde version. "I guess I do like the way the Lorde version is used nowadays," he says. "I just think that's far more epic. So I think I'm more of a fan of that."

So after hearing her version, did the band ever go back and consider reworking the song live, as Springsteen has done with "Born in the U.S.A."?

"I think between the two versions, it's perfect," he says. "I'm very, very happy."

CHAPTER TWENTY-THREE

FLEETWOOD MAC

✦ "BIG LOVE" ✦

Fleetwood Mac's "Big Love," the first single from the band's 1987 *Tango in the Night* album, was a worldwide chart success, hitting the top ten in Belgium, Ireland, the Netherlands, and the UK, as well as number five on the Billboard Hot 100 and number two on the Billboard Mainstream Rock Airplay chart. But there is one chart statistic for "Big Love" that stands out: number seven on the Billboard Dance Club Songs chart.

Looking back on that fact, which shows the song's universal appeal, the song's writer, Lindsey Buckingham, now chuckles at that anomaly. "I didn't exactly remember that," he says. "Well, who knows back then? I don't think I was paying a lot of attention to the charts by then. Maybe I was sort of taking the anticharts stance."

Or maybe, it is much more likely that over thirty years later, Buckingham associates himself more with the live version he has done in the three decades since. The reason he chose to discuss this particular song for this book is because, as he points out, the song has changed so dramatically from the band version that everyone associates with *Tango in the Night*.

"That's an interesting song because it covers a lot of ground in terms of the evolution of the song from where it began, and where it ended up, and what it started out representing and what it ended up representing," he says.

If you've been fortunate enough to see Buckingham do the song live, you see how it has changed. Just the opening alone, from the more up-tempo beat of the band's recorded version into the dramatic, guitar virtuoso solo performance he released. He explains in incredibly detailed terms, bliss for every music geek out there, how the song morphed as a result of his leaving the band prior to the tour for that album.

"If you look at the original version of the song, which was the opening of *Tango in the Night*, it obviously was a band song, it was an ensemble piece," he says. "At some point, during the time that I had to myself to let that dust settle, and to sort of regroup, and to start thinking about another solo album, which eventually became *Out of the Cradle*, I also was rethinking a very important part of my musical presentation, which was the orchestral guitar play, which was the idea of one guitar basically doing the work of a whole track. I had been building into songs that I could adapt into that format. And 'Big Love' was really the first one."

It was on the subsequent solo tour for *Out of the Cradle* that the song's present identity was born. "So by the time I took my band of boys and girls out on the road to support *Out of the*

Cradle, and we had a ten-piece band at that point with like five guitarists, two girls and three guys, and two percussionists, and a drummer, and a keyboard player and a bassist, I was doing 'Big Love' more or less in its present live form," he says. "And that was just transforming the basic idea of it, and stripping everything away, everything, and coming up with a part which would carry the whole song. And it was so effective, my performance, that I realized that that was something that I had to continue to try to look into and to have represented on solo work."

The impact of how he performed "Big Love" live, and still does, resonates on everything he does musically to this day. "It's just become something I've always wanted to try to do. And 'Big Love' was kind of the spearhead for all of that, and it's ironic because it's not like 'Never Going Back Again,' which was a single guitar, but didn't really push the envelope per se in terms of how aggressive it was or how complete it was as a single piece; it was far more demure," he says. "And so that was just something which became a really important element, and the irony being that it started off as a single ensemble piece and then transformed into something completely different."

Although the tumult in Fleetwood Mac was strong enough he felt compelled to leave the group before the *Tango in the Night* tour, he is still fond of the group version of "Big Love."

"I was quite happy with the ensemble version, the single version that was on the album. I had no designs on making it anything other than what it was at the time that we recorded it. It was just after the fact and putting myself in sort of a post–Fleetwood Mac environment where I started to get back in touch with things that had preceded Fleetwood Mac," he says.

So, in a way, the evolution to "Big Love" was also a nod to the past he and bandmate/girlfriend Stevie Nicks shared before they joined Fleetwood Mac and made music history with *Rumours*.

"And quite honestly, if you go back to *Buckingham Nicks*, you can find elements of that kind of playing on 'Frozen Love' or 'Stephanie,' or even a couple of the other songs. Much of that had to be put aside in order to do what was appropriate in the context of Fleetwood Mac," he says. "And so, there was something that I had certainly given up in order to be a member of Fleetwood Mac, there were other things that I took on—being the musical visionary or the producer, the musical leader, taking on the duties that were needed, the clarity I had, the ability to do and they had probably needed for quite some time. So it was a trade-off that I was willing to make. But, having again taken leave of the band, it was a kind of a circular mentality of sort of going back to an earlier set of impulses that I maybe had put on the shelf for a long period of time."

For anyone who has followed the highly volatile history of the most famous lineup of Fleetwood Mac—Buckingham, Nicks, Christine McVie, John McVie, and Mick Fleetwood—it is no surprise to hear Buckingham speak of sacrifice to join the band and continued turmoil. If and when the story of Fleetwood Mac is ever turned into a music biopic, the *Rumours* recording session alone would need to be minimum six hours.

"Big Love," as the lead single from *Tango in the Night*, is directly tied into that volatility. As Buckingham explains, that was a tumultuous time in the Mac history, ultimately leading to his departure.

"*Tango in the Night*, by the way, was ripe with its own kind of adversity, which was different from what we experienced during the making of *Rumours*. I've probably mentioned it to you before, [but] during the making of that album, everyone else in the band was sort of hitting critical mass with their alcohol and substance use, and it was creating a very chaotic and unstable environment within the band in terms of really being able to rely on anyone at any given time," he says. "We probably spent close to a year making *Tango in the Night*. And we made it at my house, which resonates with 'Big Love' as well. But it was made under circumstances where out of that year we probably saw Stevie for a few weeks. And Mick couldn't drive home at night, so he was living in the trailer in my front yard."

While they were able to finish the album, Buckingham didn't feel he could continue on with that lifestyle on the road. "But when it came time to tour, that craziness that the other four . . . And I am not saying I wasn't drinking, and sort of partaking, but it was a question of degree," he says. "And the other four were pretty much out of control at that point. And I did not want to be a part of that on the road, which is usually about times ten from what the studio is. And that's when I took leave of the band, and so they got Rick Vito and Billy Burnette to replace me, and went out and did their tour."

Looking back at the lyrics of the song decades later, as he reminisces on the hectic recording session, Buckingham says one line sticks out to him. "The line ending 'Big Love,' the house on the hill, that was the house where I had lived since 1981, and where I had my small studio in what had been a garage, and it was where we cut *Tango in the Night*," he says. "And it was also the house on the hill where I had not been looking for love, which is what a lot of people assume that line means. I was looking out for love, I was sort of guarding against love because not just Stevie, but other experiences which were difficult and then trying in the process of trying to maintain a love relationship. And so at that point, I was sort of a loner, and was dating girls, but I wasn't seeing anyone seriously. And I think I was just in that house on that hill, just sort of guarding against love. But in that moment, that was the space I was in."

As he talks about the subtext of the lyrics and the deep emotional vulnerability in there, the resonance of the song live comes into focus. Beyond the phenomenal and forceful guitar playing, there is an honesty in the song. And to Buckingham it's that combination of qualities the fans are responding to.

"They were reacting to the musicianship, I think, they were reacting to the raw kind of emotion of the way I was interpreting it, which was way more aggressive than on the recording, and they were reacting to just the dynamic of it and the guttural place it ends up and this really abrupt ending," he says of the live version. "And I think it just drew people in on, again, on the musicianship level, but almost on a theatrical level as well."

Ask any artist and they will tell you the evolution of a song is organic based on a variety of factors: time and distance from when the song was written and what it's about, audience response, life experience. In short, songs take on a life of their own. And Buckingham absolutely agrees that's what happened with "Big Love."

"I think that's what happened. Obviously, I had an idea where I was trying to express a faction of my musicianship in a way, but beyond that, it was just arriving at the notion of taking that song and seeing if it would work. And once I put those two things together, the song did sort of lead me in that direction," he says. "That's what creativity does most of the time. Especially when you are working alone as I do with solo work most of the time, where it's very much like painting. There's no verbalizing; it's all quite subconscious and you start throwing colors on the canvas and the words start to lead you in the direction that it wants to go, which is really cool."

Another factor in a song's metamorphosis over time is hearing and seeing how other artists interpret your work, whether it's through the many cover versions or being used in TV and film and seeing a great director utilize your song. Buckingham had the opportunity to see longtime friend Oscar-winner Cameron

Crowe utilize "Big Love" in the severely underrated *Elizabeth-town*, starring Orlando Bloom and Kirsten Dunst.

"I loved how he used that in *Elizabethtown*. I love Cameron because he's always been such a supporter of mine, and he's used a few things of mine in his films, and he gets it, so I know he's always gonna use it in a context which is completely great," he says. "And one which probably will elevate the song in some level. It's just going to create sort of a broader context for it."

He is equally flattered by the dozen or so covers that have been done of "Big Love" over the years. To him, anyone covering a song is a great compliment. "That's another way where you obviously know that I've done something right, if someone else wants to reinterpret it," he says. "You're passing a torch of sorts. That's kind of what music is for."

Buckingham admits that with all the turmoil in the making of *Tango in the Night*, which would be the last studio album to feature all five members of the *Rumours* lineup, with Buckingham, Nicks, and Christine McVie all missing from various later works, he does have a hard time reflecting on "Big Love" and its lasting legacy in pop culture.

"I think it's almost harder for the artist or the creator of a work to be objective about that kind of thing. I think other people who take it in are gonna have more insights into that and in that particular context, in that particular time frame, quite honestly, because that album was so difficult to make, and we did get through it, we triumphed and it was a great album despite all those difficulties and the chaos that was being created by the behavior of the members; I think by the end of it I was psychologically distanced from any sort of outcome," he says. "So I honestly did not pay a whole lot of attention to that because it wasn't long after finishing the album that I had to confront the band with the fact that I wanted to take leave. So I kind of put it behind me and didn't look back, and I think the finer points of the success of 'Big Love' as a single or just how it's been taken in, it kind [of] got left in the dust for me a little bit, at that point."

That is totally understandable under the circumstances. But then it is fascinating that of all of his numerous songs, he did choose "Big Love" to speak about. And it shows how the song, though associated with such a difficult and frenzied time in his life and career, has survived in his world.

"I put that version of the song and the context of it in the band behind me, but somehow I still wanted to hold on to the song and to make it a part of my pivot into a new phase of my career and my creative life, and I think it did serve as that, for sure," he says.

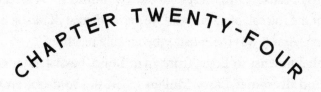

CHAPTER TWENTY-FOUR

U2

✦ "ONE" ✦

Since its release thirty years ago on the Grammy-winning album *Achtung Baby*, U2's powerful "One" has become an unquestioned modern classic. It is a staple of both pop culture and the band's live show. And since the Irish quartet has three of the top thirteen grossing tours of all time—including the second biggest tour ever, 2009 to 2011's U2 360° Tour—the song has been played thousands of times in huge settings, often to fifty thousand people or more.

But there are two performances that stand out according to guitarist Edge. The first was one the band did live. The second was one they were not even there for.

"When we performed at Madison Square Garden in the period after 9/11, we were the first band of our kind or size to perform in the city," he recalls. "And we were trying to figure out how we could honor the victims of 9/11 so we thought, *A roll call of names, it's obvious*. So we got our production designer and show designer, really got together with our people, and we had the screens because it was that era of video reinforcement screens. So we put the roll call of names and we performed at Madison Square Garden. And it was the most unbelievable reaction."

Unbeknownst to Edge, front man Bono, bassist Adam Clayton, and drummer Larry Mullen Jr., in the sold-out crowd of nearly twenty-one thousand fans, there were several men and women who'd been on the front lines of the fallen Twin Towers of the World Trade Center.

As Edge recalls, the song and the show understandably became about the heroes fighting to save lives on 9/11. "There were a lot of first responders there as it turned out; we didn't know that. And I guess they just understood that we were trying to find some way to respond," he says. "So they all came up after the show, and I think 'One' may well have been the last song. And we just let them come onstage, dozens of them, and gave them the stage and they took the microphone and they all just told their stories and it was so cathartic. It was just one of those unbelievable things to be part of. So that's hard to beat in terms of a moment where a song just fits a situation, which could only have been brought about by a song."

That is, though it may sound clichéd or corny, the true power of music: to unite and uplift twenty-one thousand people hurting, grieving, suffering, and mourning loved ones, their city, their safety, their security. And "One" is one of the few songs in history that has that as, Edge puts it, "gravitas."

"Nothing else could have unlocked that moment and created that platform for that sort of cathartic experience for these first responders but also for the whole city and certainly for us. We were so humbled by it. So that would be a big moment," he says.

Then the second performance, the one the band wasn't even part of, is also a true testament to the song's incredible emotional, worldwide reach. It came after the tragic 2020 murder of French schoolteacher Samuel Paty, who was killed following reports he showed cartoons of the prophet Muhammad to his students.

"The song was used in a funeral when the teacher who had been killed in Paris, because he had opened up a conversation about prejudice and the prophet Muhammad, and some of his pupils who were Muslims got offended," Edge says. "And I think he had mentioned *Charlie Hebdo* and that whole issue, which is huge in France. So this poor teacher was murdered by a kid, and his family asked that 'One' would be used at this funeral and they play the entire song. But I think it was the military, who were the honoree coffin bearers, and they took it as a challenge. So they worked out this whole choreography to the song and it is just incredible to see. It goes on and on and on and they go through the entire song. And it became actually the sort of the center-piece of the funeral service and we're like, 'Oh wow.'"

For Edge, to see a song they wrote thirty years ago take on that sort of role in the life of anyone, let alone Samuel Paty, is unbelievably humbling. "And again it's utterly unlinked to have something that you worked on in your little small studio all those years ago, taking on that sort of role for people and that significance," he says.

That the song would take on that role during the memorial for Samuel Paty is fitting in a way though. It was born in part out of honoring another fallen activist, Edge explains.

"When we were working on the lyric we were very inspired by a New York artist called David Wojnarowicz," he says. "And David, as well as being as a cutting-edge experimental artist, died from AIDS. So as Bono's working on the lyric, we're kind of summoning up an imagined conversation that could have happened to any one of us had we been in David's shoes. But it's, and I know everything, Bono, a lot of his personal relationships or his relationship with his father went into that lyric, so there's this conflict in it."

In Edge's estimation, that conflict Bono placed in the lyrics is a big part of what makes the song so special and enduring after three decades.

"It's not happy clappy, 'let's all hold hands around the campfire' lyric at all. Actually there's some deep hurt is revealed in that lyric and that's why it's so fascinating when people tell me, 'We played it at our wedding.' I'm going, 'Did you listen to the lyric?'" he says, laughing. "This is not a perfect, harmonious sort of situation. This is like overcoming deep hurt, deep historic problems to reach in some sort of defiant, heroic way towards this ideal of unity against all odds. That's, I suppose, why it still has that power and that connection."

"One" hasn't endured only with fans and the band. Though U2 won the Grammy for Record of the Year in back-to-back years, for "Beautiful Day" and "Walk On" (making them one of only three acts, alongside Roberta Flack and Billie Eilish, to accomplish that feat), "One" is consistently rated in polls as the greatest U2 song.

It placed thirty-sixth on *Rolling Stone*'s 2004 list of five hundred greatest songs ever, in 2003, influential British magazine *Q* named it the greatest song of all time, VH1 declared the track to be the second-best song of the nineties, and it was named by the Rock & Roll Hall of Fame as one of the five hundred songs that shaped rock 'n' roll.

Just as much as critics have loved the song, the band's peers have shown the same reverence and awe for "One." Axl Rose once famously told *RIP Magazine* that "One" is "one of the greatest songs that has ever been written."[1]

The number and talent of artists who have covered "One" over the years is astonishing. Among the artists who have performed their own version of "One" are Pearl Jam, Damien Rice, Cowboy Junkies, Chris Cornell, the legendary Johnny Cash, the Royal Philharmonic Orchestra, Joe Cocker, Adam Lambert, and the cast of *Glee*, among others.

U2 themselves have done several memorable collaborations on the song, dating back to 1993, when they teamed with members of R.E.M. to do the song at an MTV concert celebrating the inauguration of then president Bill Clinton. They also rerecorded it in 2006 with R&B great Mary J. Blige. Edge has enjoyed listening to all of these greats offer their interpretation of "One."

"They're all fascinating because when you have a song as sort of complete and crystalline in form and content as 'One' it sort of allows itself to be interpreted in different ways," he says. "And Mary J.'s vocal and passion she brings to it is amazingly moving. And Damien's version is really him but it's beautiful. It's always great to hear it in somebody else's [voice] and the emotion that they can bring to it is always fascinating."

There is one version that shines to him as being special and unlocking a different side of the song. "The one that I also loved was performing with Pavarotti and a full orchestra with Bono and [Brian] Eno," he says. "Because that sort of wide sweep, orchestral sweep, we wrote the songs very humble. It was very stripped down and very simple. And even the album version, is all the sounds are a very kind of human scale and there's nothing grandiose about it at all. But in this instance we kind of went for it and the arranger did an amazing job with this orchestra. And that was probably the one that's the biggest contrast to the original version. And it worked. It's not rock 'n' roll at all, but it worked really well."

To understand the pliability of the song and why it's able to transcend genres and audiences, to be performed by great opera singers, R&B vocalists, rock bands, and more, one needs to go back to the beginning of the writing of the song in Berlin, during the sessions for *Achtung Baby*.

Reflecting on the song, Clayton says, "I guess 'One' was another song that happened relatively quickly and we just went, 'Okay, this is bigger than all of us.'"[2]

So does Edge remember it the same? Did he know the band had come upon something that would sit one day between Bob Marley's "No Woman No Cry" and the Doors' "Light My Fire" on a greatest songs of all time list?

"Whoa," he says, almost taken aback. "I'm not sure we had a crystal ball that accurate."

However, the song came at an important point for the band, and they quickly realized it was something special. "I tell you what, it was a very timely thing during those sessions in Berlin for what became *Achtung Baby* because we'd hit a bit of a brick wall," he recalls. "We were with Daniel Lanois and led by myself; we were trying to introduce a new, more rhythmic sensibility into our music because it just seemed like we needed to develop in that regard. I felt instinctively that we could swing it if we kind of got the right material. So we were in that process of trying to write our way, as it were, to some more rhythmic tunes. And it was tough and the songs weren't finished. And so we were doing two things at the same time, trying to do rhythmic material, but unfortunately the songs weren't very convincing."

When the genesis of what would become "One" started, Edge was actually working on what would become another U2 hit song. "So in the midst of this I'm trying to work on the chorus for what became 'Mysterious Ways.' We've got a fantastic verse, we've got all these great sounds, it's rhythmic, it's happening, but it's not a song," he says. "So I'm trying to convince everyone that this is going to be a great song and Daniel Lanois was like sympathetic but uncertain and Adam and Larry are not impressed.

So I go in the other room, and this is like about the fourth attempt to try and come up with a chorus for 'Mysterious Ways.' And I come back in the room, with these two ideas. I'm like, 'Okay, look, let's try this real simple, just go in the room, we'll just go from our verse.' I play option A and it's like A minor to D to F to G. And I say, 'Okay, now, option two C, A minor, F to C.' And they're all kind of looking at me going, 'Well, maybe it'll work.'"

Edge credits Lanois with figuring out how to make the song work. "Then Danny says, 'Edge, play those together like one into the other.' So I played these two sequences together, and it was something about just the way these chords flowed," he says. "I did this in the control room on an acoustic guitar and everyone just went, 'That does sound really good; that sounds really good. Let's just forget about "Mysterious Ways." Let's just go into the room together.' And we just start playing these ideas. So I wrote the chords out for Adam and Bono. Actually, he wasn't on guitar. He was just singing. So we went in the room, we just started playing this for a while and as we're playing it, everyone starts to feel this sort of gravitas to these changes and this piece of music started to come alive. Bono got on the microphone, started improvising melodic ideas and even a few lyric ideas were coming as he was singing. So after about fifteen minutes of this we sort of came in the room and we started listening to the moments that had occurred in this improvisation. And within like another hour or so we basically had the music of that song figured out."

While the music came quickly, the lyrics did not come as easily, as Edge recalls. "Lyrically it took quite a bit longer to unlock the emotion that was in the melody and the chords and the music," he says. "And it was so timely because our band was going through such a difficult time at that moment. And it sort of was autobiographical to some extent, in that it was a kind of a call to ourselves, you know as a band as much as it was a call to inspire anyone else. So it answered a question on a couple of fronts, for us. And definitely as we left Berlin that was by far the thing we were most excited about."

Edge's original vision morphed in what was truly a collaborative manner, with both the band and producers Eno and Lanois. "This is what Eno picked up, I think, when he was suggesting we try and develop the arrangement away from its real simple, humble acoustic guitar, was that it's complicated," he says. "We did have to deconstruct the song a bit in Ireland because our first version was very acoustic driven. It was very sort of classic ballad and didn't really have some of the duality that we ended up developing when we were back in Dublin. But the song itself was there really within fifteen minutes, in terms of the emotional weight, the gravitas, the sense this is a song that is a ballad, but it's a fast song."

To Edge, it's that duality that instantly made the song a favorite during the band's live shows. Looking back on the first performances, which date to opening night of the ZOO TV Tour in Lakeland, Florida, February 29, 1992, Edge recalls it was an immediate fan favorite.

"It was. I don't mean people were punching the air or jumping around going crazy but there's a thing that you know when you're playing a great song. And it's an emotional unity that it can create in a very nonintimate space," he says. "And everything about that song had that weight and that power so yeah, we felt that very early on when we played it live. And it became like a huge number in that *Achtung Baby*/ZOO TV indoor and outdoor show. And it's one of those songs that it's a ballad but it fills an arena, fills a stadium. It brings people, it connects people. That's what's so extraordinary about the song."

As Edge recounts all these stories about the song, it quickly becomes clear there are so many extraordinary things about this track, including the organic nature of the final guitar solo. It was from that collaborative deconstruction, as Edge calls it, that the final guitar solo emerged.

"We ended up dumping the acoustic guitar and we all ended up contributing; Brian and Danny contributed a great sort of keyboard duet and I did a rhythm part, Danny did a rhythm part, and the file guitar was the ending of the song," he says. "We're literally running out of time in the studio, there is no time to do anything and we're kind of against the gun and as I'm listening to Bono doing his last vocal and I know they're about to mix it, I just happen to hit on this guitar part for the ending. I'm like, *This is gonna go down like a lead balloon; they're going to hate this*. So I went into the control room after he'd finished. 'Look, I know we're about to take the tapes.' And I was the one who took them to LA to be mastered. I said, 'Look, there's this guitar part. I have to try it.' I played the part once and it is a part I played ever since. It's the final coda on the guitar and I couldn't imagine the song without it. But it was such a spontaneous thing. And that's how the whole album and record came together. It was very much kind of just following inspiration."

But maybe the most remarkable thing about "One" is how it literally changed the world. U2 have always believed in, and spoken about, the power of a song to change the world. But "One" truly did that because of the way it altered history for lead singer Bono.

"I've only just thought about it this second, but that was really the beginning of Bono's engagement with AIDS, which became this incredibly important part of his life's work," Edge says. "And you might argue that that song was really the kind of the catalyst for an incredibly major work of his in activism and politics."

CHAPTER TWENTY-FIVE

SHANIA TWAIN

✦ **"YOU'RE STILL THE ONE"** ✦

Shania Twain's "You're Still the One" is one of the most acclaimed and beloved songs of the nineties. The soft, tender ballad won Grammy Awards in 1999 for Best Country Song and Best Female Country Vocal Performance and was nominated for Record and Song of the Year (losing both to Céline Dion's "My Heart Will Go On" from the juggernaut film *Titanic*). It also won a slew of country awards and songwriting honors, and VH1 named "You're Still the One" the forty-sixth best song of the nineties, one of several decade-end lists to honor the track.

So with that pedigree, surely Twain and her friends, family, and team knew the song would be special, right?

"I would say no because everyone seemed more enthusiastic about my energy songs. And I think that they probably see me more that way too, because I'm kind of hyperactive and I talk fast and when I have something to say I have a lot of it to say," she explains. "Label and friends and everything, they always gravitated more toward the stomping stuff or the stuff with more attitude 'cause I am very expressive."

By the time she released "You're Still the One," Twain had established that her most successful material was her boot-stomping music you line-danced to in bars across America. She had hit the top of the US country charts with "Any Man of Mine" and "(If You're Not In It For Love) I'm Outta Here!"

However, she had shown with songs like "God Bless the Child" that she could display her softer side. And if you ask her, the romantic side of "You're Still the One" is closer to the real her.

"There's this other introspective songwriter side of me that is more quietly expressive. So that's why I say a song like 'You're Still the One' is much more of who I feel I am as me, the person I know as myself," she says. "There are two different expressions in my personality that are strong. 'You're Still the One,' I guess, is the one that I identify the most with."

Given how much the song is true to her character, it is not surprising that Twain says the song came organically to her. "I felt that it was a very me, a very true to me song to be recording. So it was one of the most natural songs to write and to record," she says. "Just really something that rolled off effortlessly. And I don't know whether that makes a song more likely to succeed or not, but it certainly makes it a very honest and pure experience when you're doing it. You don't adopt a persona or mood or whatever. It's just at its core very me."

Still, even she admits that as naturally as it came to her that didn't mean she would have a worldwide hit. "We don't know, that's what I'm saying. I wouldn't have known, just because I felt so at ease with it, that that would mean that it would be a big song," she says.

As Twain recalls the writing more than two decades later, she says it came from her introspective place. "If I'm bored—and I get bored quickly—my go-to is my guitar. And that is how songs like 'You're Still the One' are written. For me, they always start in solitude," she says. "My songwriting time is always intimate. I love to be alone when writing, that's my me time. Sitting with my guitar, just playing around like a kid with a crayon box and paper. It's not so much about expressing your personality at the beginning. It's more, for me, just expressing emotions through music. Expressing them musically. So that's what 'You're Still the One' is."

Because the song wasn't her usual get-out-and-party hit and those around her weren't sure the song was right to be a single, the song's success was especially rewarding for Twain.

"What was validating about it for me personally, because I like that word as well, is when it started to become successful. It's like, 'Wow, this is really who I identify with the most, as a music artist.' It's the solitary time that yields a song like 'You're Still the One,' an intimate song like that," she says. "Because when I'm writing fast stuff and fun stuff and stuff with personality and character and attitude, I get into a different frame of mind to do that. And it isn't my go-to state of mind when I'm being creative. It just validated that, wow, people actually like that kind of stuff too that I do."

There are a lot of ways she knew the song was becoming successful, and her trust of sharing her intimate side would be rewarded. There are the awards, the chart success, fan stories, and then there is Prince covering your song and Elton John singing it back to you in a hallway. That's when you know you have an anthem for the ages.

"I heard a version by Prince as well. That was one of his favorite songs. It was very Prince-esque. It was very Prince. It was so obviously Prince. And that version made the most impact on me. I realized that, wow, really this song could live anywhere genre-wise and style-wise," she says.

Hearing his version changed the song for her in ways because it showed her the versatility of her own song. "The two most impressive, drastically different versions of the same song that I think always influenced me, in writing songs that could stand the test of time for many reasons and live many lives, was 'Layla,' done by the same artist [Eric Clapton] twice, and like they're completely different songs almost," she says. "And then you've got 'I Will Always Love You.' Completely different planets as far as productions and stylistically and everything and genre. Between Dolly [Parton] and Whitney [Houston]. So I always aspire to write music that could do that."

As Twain points out, the song has been covered many times. But Prince is another level. "A lot of people have covered it and promoted it as one of the things that they're doing. But Prince was just doing it like he does. And that just blew me away," she says. "And the other encounter with 'You're Still the One' that I'll never forget is [when] I crossed Elton John in a radio station hallway. We were both doing promo tours and I'd never met him before. And he was walking toward me, and he just starts singing 'You're Still the One.' And it was just like, wow, this song is part of my identity now. It was his way of sharing how he felt about the song and his admiration for whatever I do. And really, that meant a lot to me because he's one of my music heroes. So that was huge for me. It was like this in-person, a cappella dedication. It was incredible."

For all the awards and sales, most artists will tell you that writing a song that speaks to their peers is the greatest compliment there is. So when you have Prince cover your song and Elton John sing it back to you, you know you have created something truly special right there and that would be enough for most.

But in 2015, the young superstar duo of Harry Styles and Kacey Musgraves covered the song as well, helping it to reach new, younger audiences. Though Twain says she had noticed that even before their live cover, she was incredibly flattered by Styles's cover.

"I love him a lot. There's so many young people his age and even younger that I guess as becoming adults, started expressing it. And it was only then that I started realizing that, wow, even in my show, certain days of the week there'd be so many college students. And I'd be thinking, *Where are they coming from? I haven't been on tour in so long. No new music in so long,*" she says. "So I asked a few of them and they're like, 'My first concert was Shania Twain when I was six or when I was three. Or when I was eight.' And I'm thinking, *Wow, you guys are the kids that were lining up at the stage.* We had to set up special security so that kids could approach the stage. And parents couldn't come with them because it was just too many people. You'd have too many people. So we organized security to line so many kids up at a time where the parents could see them and the kids could approach the stage and I could say hello or sing to them or get them up onstage. And the kids were huge fans at that age. Obviously because their parents had exposed them to it. So it was their parents' music and their music. And then it remained their music and now they're coming back to the shows together as teenagers or college kids or whatever in groups of friends to celebrate, I guess, those moments of being their first concert. Or a lot of times it's siblings together. It's so awesome. That would have been on the Now Tour that I really started to notice that."

Just as "You're Still the One" became a part of the soundtracks to these great artists' lives, it became part of the foundation of her fans' lives. That, to Twain, has been an incredible honor.

"What is very beautiful is I like to connect with the audience in person when I'm doing shows and there are always couples having anniversaries to that song. Now you look at the beginning, I'm still meeting couples that have been married for twenty-five years, having their twenty-fifth anniversary, and twenty-five years from now they'll be having their fiftieth anniversary to it," she says. "So it's very, very special. I like to meet these people and they'll often come onstage and dance to it. Or their kids, I meet a lot of kids who say, 'My parents were married to this song,' and 'I want to get married to this song when I get married.' Beautiful stories like that and people celebrating, having anniversaries is already a celebration, making it through. But when you have a song that you take with you along the way, to me it means so much more. So that song now means to me just lasting love. And there's lots of successful stories of lasting love out there. It's got a beautiful place to live."

It was her fans' adoption of the song that saved it for her when playing the song initially became too painful. She wrote it for then husband, Robert "Mutt" Lange, the iconic producer who's worked with Def Leppard, AC/DC, and more. However, Lange cheated on Twain, ending their seventeen-year marriage in 2010.

Since the song was written for Lange, it was understandably hard for Twain to play the song live in concert in the turmoil after their divorce. "I was very happily married and I wrote the song about Mutt and it was only difficult to share later live, when we were divorced. So that's when it was really painful to sing," she says. "I'm like, 'Do we really have to include this song?' But I can't leave it out, because it's so many people's love song."

How did Twain get over the pain of singing the song live? By remembering that all those people have happy memories of the song. "That's the thing about songs, especially when you write them, you have to let them go. In the sense that they mean something different to everybody that embraces them. That song has its own unique meaning to every individual," she says. "And you don't own their experience. You wrote the song, you created it, but you don't own the way they're affected by that. It doesn't belong to you. So I had to get my head around it and say, 'Okay, this is not about me.' I'm singing it to people that carry their own value for the song. And it was out of respect for that value that flicked that switch. 'Let it go now, it's not about you, it's about what it means to everybody there in the audience.' And that felt good. You can't be selfish about it and say, 'Well, I'm never singing that song again because it hurts too bad.' It helped me to think of what it meant to everybody else."

As a fan, Twain has her own songs that have impacted her life, both as a child and as a teen, the way "You're Still the One" has for her fans. As a kid, it was hearing Michael Jackson's "Ben" that first resonated with her.

"That song made me hurt. It made me so sad. I just remember thinking that this is almost too intimate to share," she says. "There's a lot of music that I don't make into records, because I'm thinking, *Well, that's just way too personal.* And it's not even meant to be shared. It's just really what I'm doing for my own therapy I guess. Just sitting with my guitar and it's cathartic. So 'Ben' was one of those songs that really broke my heart for the whole sentiment behind it and the loneliness. I felt it so much and I was just a kid. I was a kid but it made me feel the pain. Music is powerful."

Her love song from her early days on the road is Journey's "Faithfully." "Oh my God, I was always the only girl on the road," she says. "It's too bad a girl's not singing this song, but it's okay, it's Steve Perry. And he's forgiven, he's a guy with this incredible high voice. But 'Faithfully' is a song I started living in my teens. Traveling around with bands and being on the road. I was fantasizing about being a rock star someday and living this song out. As the woman that was going to have to make those sacrifices. And you do; women have to make great sacrifices, especially the ones having the babies. So anyway, I was always moved by that song and it's been one of my favorite love songs forever."

Looking back on the success of "You're Still the One" after all this time, there have been several seminal moments in the song's history. One of those, for her, was the first time she heard the song across the globe.

"This was early on but I remember I was in France and somewhere in a little hotel way in the countryside somewhere, nowhere near a city, had the radio on and that song came on in the hotel," she recalls. "I feel like I'm supposed to be so far away from being Shania Twain, but 'You're Still the One' is playing in this very remote place and I thought, *It's so much bigger than me now.* That song just grew, it seems, to corners I've never even and may never get to. Which fascinates me as well. Because the music travels so much further than the artist."

Another big one for her was the song's Grammy nomination for Song of the Year, an honor specifically designed for the songwriter. "The Song of the Year was everything. I felt that that song represented me best. If you would imagine me as any one of my songs from its inception, what would that be stylistically, it would be a song like 'You're Still The One,'" she says. "It's almost got a lullaby-ish kind of melody. The intervals and the melody are very me, very natural and without production or anything, it would still have a strength on its own just as a song. And so, Song of the Year, and getting songwriter awards for that feels good, feels satisfying."

For all of the awards, accolades, and covers, though, it is the song's connection to her audience that means the most to Twain. "It is the coolest feeling in the world and that's what made it easier when that song no longer applied to me for the reason that I wrote it, that I was able to love it again without wanting to cry because of the wonderful feeling," she says. "I guess I would say the reward, to me, is other people's feelings for the song. And being aware of that was everything. I knew that it meant everything to them, at least in that moment. It's incredibly satisfying and also it made me realize, wow, it was so much more powerful than I ever imagined it ever would be. Just sharing my own simple, personal intimate feelings. And that so many people would share in it for their own reasons. So those are the biggest rewards, the biggest award, the biggest accolades, to me."

CHAPTER TWENTY-SIX

TOM WAITS

✦ "TAKE IT WITH ME" ✦

There are many different ways to quantify the cultural significance and impact of a song—awards, sales, streams, views. Then there is the personal impact. Tom Waits's "Take It With Me," a song from the Grammy-winning *Mule Variations* album he cowrote with wife and frequent collaborator, Kathleen Brennan, doesn't have the sales or streams perhaps of other anthems. But it is arguably the best song from one of the greatest living songwriters in music. And Waits's status as one of the greatest living songwriters is not arguable.

The first point people always make, and rightly so, when discussing Waits's cultural impact is the absolutely insane list of artists who have covered his songs: Bruce Springsteen, Rod Stewart, the Eagles, the Ramones, Johnny Cash, Céline Dion,

Hootie & the Blowfish, Sarah McLachlan, Bette Midler, Bob Seger, and countless others. The wide array of artists from different genres showcases how deeply and far his songs reach. He has collaborated with the Rolling Stones, Bonnie Raitt, Keith Richards, Preservation Hall Jazz Band, Los Lobos, and more.

Then there is the way other artists talk about him. Even if you don't know his music, he is the artist your favorite artist can't stop talking about. Jon Bon Jovi and Metallica are massive fans. Sammy Hagar once approached me at an event and said excitedly, "I didn't know you knew Tom Waits." And proceeded to hit me with a slew of questions.

I could have picked any one of a wide array of songs. "Downtown Train," which Stewart took to the top ten; "Jersey Girl," a song Springsteen has regularly done in concert; "That Feel," which Waits wrote with Richards; "Ol' 55," a hit for the Eagles. Even Waits and Brennan admit they were surprised I picked this particular song.

But there is something about "Take It With Me," a song I have long said could be played at my wedding or funeral. So for this book I decided to reach out to Waits and Brennan to ask them to include "Take It With Me" as one of my personal favorite songs. Waits rarely does interviews, but to my gleeful amazement he and Brennan agreed to participate by writing their own views on the song and songwriting. So here, in their own words, are Tom Waits and Kathleen Brennan on "Take It With Me" and songwriting.

✦ ✦ ✦

Dear Steve, We talked and wrote a bit about songwriting in general and "Take It With Me" specifically and then about the process of trying to talk about our songs and this is the result . . .

TOM WAITS: We always bury our own personal things well disguised in our songs. Perhaps it is the arrogance of believing reality can especially be improved upon at all times. If you grew up on Strube Avenue you know that Bourbon Street or Telegraph Canyon Road or Larimer Street are names with more heft, more color . . . see, the truth is so overrated. Okay, so like for example, especially in a song like "Ode to Billie Joe" . . . it has the name of counties and towns nearby, and other neighbors and kin . . . "another sleepy, dusty Delta day." They give the song a sense of place. We all have our own standards when it comes to a "good song" or a "good story." So we wanted one more tune for *Mule* and then it was done. Kathleen and I moved a piano into a hotel room and stayed there three or four days and wrote songs. We had young kids at the time and a piano and a quiet room did not exist at home. Once you know what kind of animal the song is, then the song itself can determine if it needs a cage or a saddle. We have written songs on buses, cabs, airports, trains, emergency wards, and in laundromats, dressings rooms . . . you name it . . . so what you try to do is something cinematic.

KATHLEEN BRENNAN: Memories, the feelings they conjure, are fluid and volatile, evolving and dissolving. For instance, I remember us being at home in my studio/work room, with the antique upright piano Tom found for me, us sitting and playing some phrases of notes to each other, our wandering in conversation and reverie . . . he remembers us in a hotel room. Both recollections are vivid and true . . . except mine is the correct one. Everything classifies as music: words, telephone poles, old nurse hats, feet on asphalt, an old toothbrush . . . Mystics say all is illuminated and I feel that but, for me, that light, the illumination, is music, everyone and everything is filled with it. Everyone senses it in a way particular to their winds.

TOM: We can say, I love "Moon River" . . . let's try to do something like "Moon River" as if anyone can write a lyric like Johnny Mercer. Or as if Johnny Mercer could write his lyric without Mancini. Only Johnny Mercer can write like Johnny Mercer. But it may give you a high-water mark to attempt that. For us, images like "Beaula's porch" and "Coney Island" make it dreamy. With "Take It With Me," no one was hurt in the making of it. My wife maintains that I always have to put someone in a song who has some type of handicap . . . so, this ballad has no wounded or maimed, no one has lost a finger or put an eye out or has a limp. I had to promise my wife that I would not allow anyone to get injured and I stuck to it. To most folks, when they hear the phrase *take it with me*, it is like saying, "after I am gone." And "all that you've loved is all you own" feels like you are saying that if you lovingly experience something . . . then you can take *that* with you . . . so you load up with images and memories . . . because when someone is gone that is how you bring them back.

KATHLEEN: As elaborate as a forensic may be, as hard as it tries to label, dissect, bottle, and theorize, decode, and sanitize . . . ultimately, I believe some songs, like life, remain a mystery. I like elusion and illusion; if you surrender your ideas and knowing, it's the mystery that keeps a certain poem, song, prayer, story, or romance alive; keeps you listening, seeing, watching, wondering again and again . . . and that wondering/innocence/love connects to the wonder/innocence/love that infiltrates and blossoms and pulses through you and all of life. Of course, this sublime ideal is obviously not true for every song of ours, no more than it is true for every wave of grain, Thanksgiving, first love, vacation, and on and on . . . but when you have aspirations and they survive shipping and handling and, in turn, engender a shared feeling and experience for strangers, well . . . that's a jubilation that doesn't get old.

I wonder if the words on a page alone can convey the song's heart . . . ? I need the music, the sound of the room, the places in Tom's voice, the sound of the pedals as he played the piano . . . or the sound of your voice, if you choose to sing it, to carry the words, which, in our thinking, are also the music. When I read the words, I hear the music . . . they are forever wed.

TOM: All songs are easy and hard to make, but once they are released they become part of whoever hears them or whoever loves them. Songs are like hypnotic suggestions. When you write songs with someone it is like working in the kitchen . . . "I'm gonna stick in some more garlic and basil" . . . and she goes . . . "The fuck you are . . . you will ruin it . . . go sit down."

KATHLEEN: For us, this song itself is, perhaps, how we will find ourselves and each other after we are gone. And maybe, for others, the song connects them to the love/loves that will find them and vice versa after they are gone from this life or any other life they walk into or away from.

Songs are continuum travelers/spirits and they carry listeners into that stream where the past flows into the moment and out of the moment into the future and beyond. All of those quotidian moments, lawn singing, closing down shop to just stare into each other's eyes or sharing the last French fry . . . the passing words . . . even the losses that turn the pages to discoveries . . . that is the bone Tom and I chewed on as we looked back and looked forward that day . . . yes, the song finished itself in a day. That is my memory. That is not how it goes often, as you know. Some songs Tom has recorded and released, one or both of us will still consider unfinished . . .

TOM: This was the last song we recorded for *Mule Variations*. My favorite line is, "I've worn the faces off all the cards, I'm gonna take it with me when I go."

KATHLEEN: Now, here you go . . . good example of what pulling a line from a song can do for you. That line, standing alone, makes me sad and lonely, as I think of the story that accompanies that image. But in the story of the song, it signifies, for me, getting every last drop out of the bottle. We wrestle with the riddles and paradoxes of life like everyone and most of our days are spent doing the chores we all do in hopes of keeping our worlds stitched together. Our idea of songs is sometimes to paint the story of a feeling . . . We don't believe we are the same person that returns after every departure, and that includes the Big Departure . . . so what is eternal? All those big questions put into the simple world of that small song, those tender and tiny moments . . . common to all. Tom has a natural, visceral, hand-in-earth connection to life, to songs, to faces, quirks, the peculiar . . . the people that connect to his voice hear his gnarled branches, the vulnerability of the details he uses to flesh out a tale . . . you can just hear the story and know it's true. But Tom's voice and his phrasings on the piano or a guitar unbury a deeper truth. I'm fortunate to write with him; he knows the favorite worn chair or vase or coffeepot to sit my lines into so they don't obstruct or take off without us . . . or how to take a melody or fraction of a musical release or interlude and embrace and harmonize and translate it to his phrasings or melodies or rhythms . . . he's fluent in musical conversation both historic and improvisational and intuitive.

TOM: It is like a painting and only you can decide when it is done. If the song is too personal, it will not relate. But if it has a metaphoric aroma then the listener will supply their own pictures as they are finishing the song with their own experiences and their own memories. Someone is making dinner and the flavors drift out the window and it will make someone who is walking by hungry. It does not matter that it was not for you; we all understand the rapture of a song. Like a bubble with feelings in it that floats by and breaks open near your ear.

TOM AND KATHLEEN: "Take It With Me" is one of the songs that still holds up for us. We just listened to it for the first time in a long time after you asked about it. We can still feel its vulnerability. And the aging of the song and of us has not changed that feeling. The feeling, the sentiments of the song were meant to be true for then and now. Even if there are no phones to take off the hook . . . the sentiment still translates. Frankly, it is baffling (in a not unpleasant way), that this small, intimate, and widely unknown song is one you asked about. We thought you must be doing a book on your favorite obscure songs. When we got the list of songs you were writing about it seemed preposterous to place this among the wildly popular, iconic songs you picked . . . We feel, like you said . . . the song could be invited to a wedding or a funeral . . . a birth . . . a breakup or a reunion . . . so perhaps, it will hold up in the company of your book.

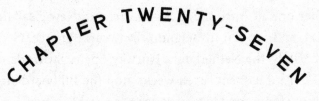

CHAPTER TWENTY-SEVEN

TLC

✦ "NO SCRUBS" ✦

Do you believe in love at first sight? TLC's Rozonda "Chilli" Thomas has definitely experienced love at first sound. As she recalls she knew the instant she heard the opening of the group's 1999 smash "No Scrubs" the song was going to be a classic.

"Listen, I remember being at the studio and the producer, Kevin 'She'kspere' Briggs, came there, he wanted to get on the album. We were almost done with *FanMail*. And he was playing some songs and stuff, and I was just listening, and then when I heard the beginning, I was like, 'Oh.' It caught my ear immediately, and I didn't even have to get to the hook," she says. "I said, 'I need to do that. I'm doing this one right here. When can we get in the studio?' And we were in the studio probably like two days later, and I knocked it all out, the backgrounds, everything, the harmonies, the whole thing in five hours. I knew it, I said, 'This is a hit.' I just knew it instantly."

Well, she was spot-on with her gut instinct about the song's commercial potential. "No Scrubs" became a global hit, reaching number one in Australia, Canada, Ireland, New Zealand, and Poland, and top ten in Belgium, Denmark, France, Germany, Greece, Italy, the Netherlands, Norway, Spain, Switzerland, and the UK. And it spent seven weeks atop the Billboard Hot 100, becoming the second biggest song of the year behind Cher's "Believe." It also won Grammys for Best R&B Performance by a Duo or Group with Vocal and the album, *FanMail*, won Best R&B Album.

As soon as Thomas heard the song she knew it would become an anthem of female empowerment just based on her experiences with a few scrubs in her life, she says, laughing now.

"I knew that every girl could relate to what this song is talking about. At the time, in that moment, I was just only thinking about how girls could relate to this record," she says. "'Cause some women it's like that's all they seem to attract are scrubs. I've had a couple of scrubs and that was about it. I know how to duck and dodge and weave. I know how to move out the way. I can smell a scrub a mile away."

First obvious question: What constitutes a scrub? Thomas says the answer hasn't changed in more than twenty years. "It's the same. Guys are still living at home or mooching off of somebody, having kids and you're not there, not taking care of your children, not being responsible, you don't care to get a job, you're not ambitious, all of that stuff. Sadly, it's not changing. So it just keeps going from generation to generation. It won't stop," she says with a chuckle.

So given that, as Thomas explains, women have been dealing with scrubs for years, she knew that women everywhere could relate their own life experiences to the song. What she never anticipated is the response from men.

"I didn't even think about a guy looking at it like, 'Shoot, I like this song 'cause I'm not that or I don't wanna be that,'" she says. "And so now I'm looking at it, I'm like, wow, everybody could relate to this in some way."

One of her favorite live memories of the song comes from watching as the men sang along proudly with every word.

"We performed at Drake's OVO Fest, and the majority of the people there, especially artists, they're guys from the rap world, and when 'No Scrubs' came up, they're up there singing their hearts out with us. I'm looking over like Snoop and all these people singing 'No Scrubs.' It was crazy to see," she says. "'Cause you don't expect that; you expect the girls to sing along and all that, and maybe the guys to sit this one out. No, no, no, they were singing every word and jamming."

Drake's OVO Fest is just one of many times she recalls seeing some of the biggest male pop stars in music belting out each word as their own sort of anthem.

"Even like the Jonas Brothers, all these guys, and Hanson, they sing our songs and I've heard them singing. I'm just like, it's so crazy because you got these guys singing 'No Scrubs' and not changing anything. And so that right there was amazing to me. I said, 'I can't believe this,'" she says. "And then I send it to Tionne ["T-Boz" Watkins] or our manager, I'm like, 'Did you guys see this?' And Justin Timberlake was at the studio and he was with Timbaland, and Justin was just singing 'No Scrubs.' He just started singing it."

Although Thomas never imagined "No Scrubs" becoming a favorite of men, she now understands exactly what it is about the song men relate to so strongly. "I think it could be that they just like the record, and then of course, a lot of people always have to tell you they feel comfortable singing it because they know they're not a scrub," she says. "They'll go in that direction. But it's always amazing to me. 'Cause even when Weezer did it, I was like, 'They're doing "Scrubs"?' I was surprised. It shocked me, honestly."

She sees the positive influence on men in a couple of ways. One: being proud they aren't scrubs. Or those who realize they don't want to be considered scrubs. "Well, the most stuff that we hear, and I've heard through the years, is that guys don't really wanna sit on the passenger side anymore. That was like, you don't wanna do that," she says.

But not every male response was positive. Someone wrote a rebuttal song. That's how you know you've really hit a nerve: when someone feels the need to answer your song.

"Some guys have gotten angry. Some of the lyrics may have touched them a bit," she says, laughing. "And they don't like the song, they wanna hate on it. Sporty Thievz came out with 'No Pigeons.' They had to do like a whole opposite dis for us girls. I was like, 'See, a hit dog will always holler.' And that's how we just did that, and so you do have some guys that kind of look at the song with a side-eye, but we know why."

Not only did she and her bandmates find the response song, "No Pigeons," both flattering and amusing, they approved the track. "I was like, 'You validated the point, one hundred percent. 'Cause I remember we had to approve it or something like that, we were like, 'Cool, we don't care,'" she says. "It just brought more attention to our song anyway. This struck a nerve. For you to go in the studio and come up with something completely dissing women and all this kind of stuff."

In addition to finding the dis track comical, they could also point at any negativity and say, "We have one of the biggest male artists of all time in our corner." Though one of the first times he came out to support them, the members of TLC were as surprised as the crowd, she recalls, listing some of her favorite live performances of the song.

"When we performed at MTV, and we actually had the swings, like the actual video itself. And then another time we performed—now this was crazy—we had no idea that Prince was gonna introduce us. It was a surprise, and he introduced us, and he said, 'TLC, my favorite group,'" she says, the amazement still in her voice all these years later. "We're like, 'What?' We couldn't believe it. It's like, 'No way. Did you hear what he said?' It was crazy. We got no warning or anything, we had no idea that he was gonna introduce us, and what he was gonna say."

For anyone who was lucky enough to know Prince or be in his inner circle, it isn't unusual to hear how he liked to surprise people. Introducing them onstage without their knowledge wasn't even the biggest surprise he sprung on TLC. That came during a concert.

"We're at Madison Square Garden, and he just came out of the blue and had the guitar, and we're performing and we're like looking and we're like, 'Oh my God, that's Prince.' And he was just onstage, just playing the guitar to our songs while we're performing. It was wild. I'm telling you," she says. "We didn't know. I get he wanted to just come up and play, and he did. Who is gonna say no to the great Prince? You want him onstage with you and he didn't practice. He was a genius and he heard it and he was able to just go in. We're performing and we're like, 'Okay, to the left of us is Prince right now, like chilling, playing guitar onstage, like we've been in rehearsals and everything like, no, he just showed up and popped up here. It was crazy!'"

When you have a song that goes on to become as big a global hit as "No Scrubs" was, you often don't get the chance to appreciate it as the success is happening. It is like being in the middle of a whirlwind. So a lot of these moments, like Prince coming out and jamming with you by surprise, you don't get to fully appreciate until years later.

But now, twenty-plus years later, Thomas has so many of those moments to reflect on. Among the ones she is proudest of is how the song has carried on to younger generations.

"When you have other artists singing it 'cause that's why their fans are coming to see them and everybody is singing it. We've seen that so many times and I'm just like, 'Oh my gosh, this is crazy.' And then you see movies and it's just like, 'Oh, it's here,' or it's in a TV show or something like that, and it just kind of keeps going. It's almost like it takes a life of its own to become what you're saying, that anthem," she says. "And to see little girls, even on social media, and you have these little girls—I posted this one lady, and she has her two daughters, and it's like she's teaching them and they come right in on it and they're singing it and everything. It's just crazy to see that."

It is the longevity of the song's appeal that stands out to Thomas. "To your point, you don't know if a hit is going to turn into an anthem 'cause a hit could just be for however long during that moment in time," she says. "But again, time tells you if something is gonna have longevity to it, 'cause you don't know. The years have to go by and stuff like that, people continuing, every generation catching it. It's in movies and things like that. It just keeps going, all over TikTok, such things."

Indeed, the song has enjoyed a sustained and storied popularity in Hollywood, appearing in such TV series as *Happy Endings*, *It's Always Sunny in Philadelphia*, the Netflix series *Love*, *9-1-1*, *Veronica Mars*, *Cold Case*, and even the HBO classic *The Sopranos*. When you have a song that can be used in popular sitcoms like *Happy Endings* and *It's Always Sunny in Philadelphia* and dramas such as *Cold Case* and *The Sopranos*, that song is going to hit a lot of different viewers.

The band has performed the song on *American Idol*, and the song being used on *Dancing with the Stars* also stands out to

Thomas. "I've seen it on *Dancing with the Stars*. They had a whole tribute to girl bands and things like that, and they did a whole little thing with it and I liked it," she says.

However, it's the way the song has become cross-generational and even become an unlikely learning tool for the younger generations that pleases her the most. She hears those messages from boys and girls.

"I've had some women tell me that they let their young sons, or this one lady told me even her grandson, she let him listen to the record and say, 'These are the things that you should not do. Don't do any of this kind of stuff, so that you're not this. So a song like this does not apply to you with your actions,'" she says. "So I was like, 'Okay.' 'Cause I'll always be like, 'We gotta school the girls.' But then I'm like, 'Well, we gotta school the guys too, and be like, "Hey, don't be this guy."' So I've heard many stories like that from women telling me about them teaching their boys not to be a scrub. And I support that 'cause I have a son too. And I tell him, 'I'm raising you to be a certain kind of young man.'"

Ultimately, though, the song was written as a voice for women of all ages, and the educational value of the song is carrying over for women of all ages. Thomas says it's because there will always be scrubs. There will always be women who need to be reminded to treat themselves better.

"To me, a scrub is like a roach, right? It won't die. It just multiplies. I don't care how many years goes by, scrubs would never not exist and some guys obviously always have these traits doing these things. So when a song is that relatable, especially when it comes to those dynamics between men and women or whatever, it just sticks with you," she says. "It can always hang around because these experiences are always gonna happen. You know what they say: it's the same game, it's just new players," she adds, laughing.

And nothing brings her more joy than when she hears from little girls they are adopting the song and its mantra into their lives. And more than twenty years later she still hears that all the time.

"Honestly, they just tell me that they love it. They love the song. It's their favorite song or whatever or one of their favorite songs. And it's mostly from little girls," she says of the messages she gets about the song today. "Some of their parents will tell me, 'Tell her what's your favorite song.' And they say, 'No Scrubs.' And when they say that, I'm like, 'Good, listen to the lyrics. Make sure you stay away from guys like that,'" she says, cracking up.

CHAPTER TWENTY-EIGHT

LINKIN PARK

✦ "IN THE END" ✦

ore than two decades after its release, Linkin Park's debut, *Hybrid Theory*, remains the best-selling rock album of the twenty-first century. The band's guitarist and co-songwriter Brad Delson believes that is a testament to the album's quality from top to finish. "I think every song on that album is really strong," he says.

The album spawned four singles: "One Step Closer," "Crawling," "Papercut," and the final one, "In the End." "I think 'In the End' stands out even among them," Delson says.

The song's success upon release bears that out. While the first two singles both hit the top five on multiple Billboard rock charts, including the Alternative Airplay, Mainstream Rock Airplay, and Rock and Metal, "In the End" is the track that catapulted the band into the mainstream, hitting number two on the Hot 100 and ending the year at number seven on the year-end Hot 100.

Delson traces the song's emergence into becoming an anthem early on. "In terms of becoming an anthem, 'One Step Closer' came out, kind of put us on the map, like on MTV, then the album came out, sales never really dropped after the first week, which is very rare," he says. "We were already touring, already building a fan base, fought with our record company about what the second single would be, we thought it should be 'Papercut,' and they were a lot smarter and knew that 'Crawling' was the way to go. MTV was really important for us at that time. And if something was on MTV, kids knew it. 'Crawling' really bumped us up a whole level touring, touring, touring all the time."

According to Delson, the early success of the first three tracks set everything up so when "In the End" was released as a single on October 9, 2001, fans had become familiar with Linkin Park and were primed for the song to become a smash.

"When 'In the End' hit, it was like in top rotation on MTV, the video. There's a close-up of Chester [Bennington] that's really iconic. And so the songs being on MTV and growing, 'In the End' was the apex of pop culture attention around the album and it was like a climactic spotlight on the band," he says. "And so the power of the video being in popular culture rotation on MTV and us being on tour, basically metal tours, was a really powerful phenomenon."

The song was able to cross over into different genres, taking the band from rock and metal charts into MTV success. "I'd say the song took on a life of its own. It was on *TRL* [*Total Request Live*], which was basically really pop stuff," Delson recalls. "And so at that point, it's like you're pressing on the gas to get on the freeway and you're starting to accelerate and that song just hit its stride. At a certain point, there was no thought of, *Oh, we should promote this*. It was just like, 'Let's take our foot off the gas and it's now in orbit. There's nothing we need to do.' The song hit launch and now it's just in orbit."

Though the song would eventually become a worldwide smash, Delson doesn't recall exactly when, in the band's early days of touring, "In the End" became the sort of sing-along anthem that an entire sold-out audience screamed at the top of their collective lungs. But once the song did become a huge success he noticed the crowd responded to the track in a unique way.

"At some point, and I don't know when, the bridge of the song became the moment of the song, especially live. And that's an unusual thing in a song because the chorus is always the most memorable part, and the bridge chords are the same as the chorus," he says. "However, you get this new lift emotionally, lyrically, melodically. And that's the part, that audience, that crowds at shows really embrace. When you say *anthem*, I think of an anthem being embraced by other people as this is their story. And 'In the End,' I believe, became an anthem because of the way people relate to the whole song, and in particular, the way they sing out the bridge."

Once the song achieved its anthem status it became a centerpiece of the band's live shows around the globe, a song that fans would sing along with in the States, Europe, Asia, everywhere. And with that there were several emotional, memorable performances. But as a fan there was likely no more emotional performance than October 27, 2017, a few months after the band's singer, Chester Bennington, was found dead July 20 of that year.

On October 27, the five remaining members of the band came together with a wide array of special guests—from Alanis Morissette and Gavin Rossdale to members of Korn and System of a Down—to pay tribute to Bennington at the Hollywood Bowl.

But no guest was brought out to sing the emotional "In the End," leaving that to the capacity crowd, who poured their hearts, emotions, and tears into screaming every word of the song.

Though the emotion was at peak level that night, Delson had seen that kind of outpouring from fans at the live shows for years.

"People connect very strongly with the music, they really have embraced it as their own, have a true emotional connection with the music, with the songs, and you've seen it. There's an outpouring of connection and emotion about these songs that it couldn't be more personal for people, how they relate to these songs," he says. "You can see it on an individual level when someone's telling a story about how they connected with the song. And then you see it on a collective level in concert, when this kind of community of individuals becomes one super-loud, multidimensional voice. And the volume at which people sing, and particularly the bridge, I mean, the whole song, they'll rap all the verses. And without exception, we get to the bridge, that became a moment where not only would Chester not have to sing at all, the crowd basically became louder than the PA at that moment. And so we just stopped playing, we would stop playing the whole song at that moment, we would stop the guitars and drums, and the crowd would just sing the whole song, and then we would have the hilarious task of trying to get back in sync with the song, with ourselves. However, at that moment in the song, we didn't need to do anything. We just had to stand there and receive it."

As with all of the anthems in this book, it starts with the writing, what Delson calls "a kernel of an idea." And he remembers distinctly when "In the End" morphed from that idea to becoming a full-blown song. And it all started with being a young band making their major label debut.

"So there's that joke that you have your whole life to write your first album and then you have a month to write your second. So this was the former. Making *Hybrid Theory* was kind of the culmination of kids becoming a real band. So we carried a lot of material into *Hybrid Theory* from very early iterations of our band. We weren't even called Linkin Park. We were called Xero, and then we were called Xero 818. And then we were called Hybrid Theory. And then the label was like, 'You can't be called Hybrid Theory. There's some dance group in France or something kind of in that vein,'" he recalls. "We went through a whole process of trying to find a new name and Chester drove by this park in Santa Monica and he just thought it sounded cool."

But never happy about giving up the moniker Hybrid Theory, they made it the name of the album when they went into the studio where "In the End" was eventually born.

"We carried a lot of material into the studio at NRG with Don Gilmore, a real producer, and he was really serious about getting the most out of us and really holding us to a high standard and pushing us, pushing Mike [Shinoda] and Chester on lyrics, holding the bar really high. And I think even before that, we were just writing and writing and writing, and we felt like we had a lot of good material to bring into the studio to make a first album. And we also felt like, whether it was internal drive or encouragement, just continuing to write, and at one point, I remember it as kind of in the make-it-or-break-it kind of final hours of 'What material might we bring into the studio?'" he says.

This was, as Delson points out, in Linkin Park's pre–rock star days, well before they shared the Grammy stage with Jay-Z and Paul McCartney or headlined their own Projekt Revolution festival. So, as he recalls in vivid and colorful detail, the song's grit may have a lot to do with the space it was born in.

"Mike locked himself into our rehearsal space, which was in Hollywood, called Hollywood Rehearsal Space or something. It was like an inventive name. And not the most luxurious space in the world, but it was where we had a lockout [rehearsal space] and where we went to rehearse. And not to stay. You'd go there. You'd have to have your wits about you, 'cause that area was really dicey at that time," he says. "The woman who ran it was really sweet, and Mike found a way, basically, I don't know if he had permission or he just basically locked himself. He probably, for his own safety, had the manager of the space lock him in. And it wasn't a space you'd want to stay in at night, at all. And I don't know if he was in our room or a different room. I think he was in a different room that actually had a skylight. And he just was writing, and I think we came the next day, and we're like, 'Dude, are you okay? Did you survive?'"

Perhaps it was the pressure of the deadline, but not only did Shinoda survive, he thrived in the tough setting. "He had this burst of an idea. He had the chorus. I think he had verses. And I think we put out the original version, the original verses in the *Hybrid Theory, 20th Anniversary Edition* box set. And the verses are great in the original. And he references the skylight in that version. So, really, the verse jumped off the page, and then the chorus was just so strong," Delson recalls. "And then we kind of went about refining it with Don at NRG. At one point I remember the bassline changing in the studio, and it was very similar; however, someone played bass, and it lost the groove of the song. And I remember saying the original groove of the bass was the one. And so I actually think the bassline creates a great rhythm with the drums. And I'm really glad we got that right too. And I just love the interplay. I think it's one of the most just kind of effortless, magical interplays between the rap vocal and the sung vocal in the verses. It's just so natural how Chester overlaps the beginning of the lines, and then holds the note. It's so simple, and it's just such a perfect kind of marriage of those two things, which is certainly what our first album was all about."

Looking back now more than two decades later, no moment with the song has captured that initial purity, for Delson, of hearing it for the first time the way he did that morning in the Hollywood rehearsal space.

"For me, personally, the most magical moment is usually seeing a song come into the ether out of nowhere. That is the most amazing magic trick ever. And so probably sitting with Mike in Hollywood Rehearsal Space in the morning, kind of bleary-eyed, and hearing it for the first time, hearing the early, early kernel for the first time, that to me stands out," he says.

One of the other standout performances of the song, for him, is well after it had become a live anthem. "And then I'd say on the polar opposite, maybe one of our later tours in Europe, outside, in Italy. I think it was the end of a tour outside in the summer in Italy, and very passionate Linkin Park fans in Italy, by the way. And it was a big crowd. It was kind of a makeshift space. It wasn't a space where they have concerts. It's like, I'm gonna just put a stage in the middle of nowhere, it seemed to me. And there were probably like fifty thousand people. And I remember the singing on that song, particularly the bridge, I remember was significantly louder than the PA. The crowd singing was significantly louder than the PA. I couldn't really tell what was coming out of the PA because the crowd singing was so powerful," he says.

For Delson, that exchange between artist and fan is what they strive for. "No one wants to ever play a show and then have people not care. I'm sure you've been to shows where someone's pouring out their heart, and people just aren't paying attention, and they're having dinner or walking by. And when someone makes art, they're doing it as probably some form of expression, and ultimately, connection. And I think most artists probably want people to care about their work," he says. "And some art forms don't lend themselves to feedback. You don't get immediate feedback, when you write a novel, you might be working on it for years, and then someone reads it, or even in a movie, an actor might be on a set, pour out their heart in a scene, and then it's being edited for a year, and then it's in a theater. What's amazing about music is there's this kind of this immediate connection point with people sharing it. And live, the person who made the song potentially has the opportunity to be in the moment with an audience. And that's such an amazing blessing of an experience. And the best version of it is people investing themselves into the song, and really deeply more than caring, making it their own, and that becoming a real form of connection."

Not only has he seen that connection live, but he has heard the stories from fans directly for years. Linkin Park were famous for their accessibility with their audience. They did meet and greets before every show, no matter how big they got. So he got to talk to the fans and hear from them why the song meant so much.

"At any given meet and greet, you might hear multiple people say that. I think the emotion I get on a visceral level from that song is catharsis. And I think there's no greater version of it than seeing that song played live when as a collective, there's a collective catharsis," he explains. "And you even described it at the Hollywood Bowl, what you just said. It's a conduit for emotion. And certainly, Chester was so emotionally available and so real, that it's just an opportunity for people to pour their hearts out."

To Delson, the song's continued success and appeal is a testament to the unique bond Linkin Park shared with their fans, who were dubbed the Linkin Park Soldiers. And while many of the band's hit songs over the years had that bond with the fan base, perhaps none had quite the same emotional pull as "In the End" possessed.

"I'm super grateful to my bandmates, my teammates, my friends for the journey, and for the camaraderie and for the real creative partnership. What's amazing about Linkin Park is the sum is bigger than the parts. So it's like all of our collective talents and energy poured into this creative adventure. And ultimately one that became even greater because of the outpouring and collaboration with our fan base. As great as the song is, the song doesn't become what it is today without the audience and other people connecting with the music and making it their own," he says.

Even he can't say exactly why this particular song has such a resonance with fans, some of whom were not even alive when *Hybrid Theory* was first released.

"What I noticed recently is kids who are teenagers are discovering our music, maybe *Hybrid Theory*, maybe *Minutes to Midnight*, maybe *Meteora*, albums that were certainly made even before they were born. *Hybrid Theory, 20th Anniversary Edition*, we rereleased it and it was an amazing box. And to me, what was the most compelling about *Hybrid Theory, 20th Anniversary Edition* wasn't, 'Oh, here's a nostalgia thing from twenty years ago.' I've been hearing kids who are sixteen say, 'This is my favorite album.' Right now, today. So the question is: Why is it so relevant, maybe even more relevant today, twenty years later?" he asks. "How did that happen? I don't know that. I have no idea. [But] I think that's really interesting and I think that's a really cool lineage to be a part of because I can tell you when I was fourteen, two of my favorite bands were the Doors and Led Zeppelin. And I wasn't alive when *Led Zeppelin IV* came out, but I had the Led Zeppelin songbook and was learning every Led Zeppelin song on guitar."

Ask any artist in this book and they will tell you there is no formula for writing an anthem. Because if there were they would all do it with every song. But years later, as an artist, you can step back and maybe detach yourself from it a bit and figure out why a song started on its journey to becoming an indelible part of pop culture. That's where Delson is today with "In the End."

"I think it's a great song. I think that's the power of a great song. I think it's well written. I think the words, the melodies, the emotional performance, the musical bed I think is beautiful. I think if you just listen to the track that would also probably be compelling. I think all of the elements conspire together to connect," he says. "And yeah, I think it's inspiration, I think it's luck, I think it's focus on being in the studio and getting the recipe right. Someone might have a burst, and then it's really refining it. Even the mix, even all the details like being in New York with Mike and working with Andy Wallace on the mix, the mastering. A song has so many layers and so many parts. I'm just thinking about the song and the feeling of it. I think everyone invests in the best version of a piece of art, particularly a song. Someone has an opportunity, if they hear something, to really invest themselves into the story, and it becomes their own. And that's what I've seen happen with 'In the End.' I'm grateful."

CHAPTER TWENTY-NINE

MY CHEMICAL ROMANCE

✦ "WELCOME TO THE ✦
BLACK PARADE"

*M*ost songs, no matter how big they become, have inauspicious live beginnings. Typically the song was played first before it was released, as Grace Slick detailed with "White Rabbit," to an audience totally unfamiliar with it. Or on rare occasion, the song is a hit before it is played live, so the audience knows the song and sings along from the outset, as U2 experienced with "One."

But no song in this collection had a more interesting debut live performance than My Chemical Romance's 2006 anthem "Welcome to the Black Parade."

"The first time we played that song was an extremely awkward experience. The first time we had ever played it, really, in a live sense was for the VMAs [Video Music Awards], and MTV was like, 'Well, we have no room in the show proper, but you guys could play a song before the VMAs start,'" My Chem front man Gerard Way recalls. "And we had all agreed, 'Okay, we're gonna play "Welcome to the Black Parade."' We rehearsed it, obviously, but we hadn't played it that much. We just played it however many times we had to practice before we did it. So you gotta picture this. We get to this building, it's a real high-rise building, we go up there, all the gear is up there. Now, there's this little very short kind of stage thing that I think they built, and they had taken the glass away from the edges, 'cause they didn't like the way it looked. So they had removed the barriers to keep you from falling off. Now, if you fell, you would have gotten seriously injured. You wouldn't have hit the pavement because there was a landing, but the landing was really far away. And I started to develop a serious fear of heights. So we're up here in this environment with all these people around too, and we had said, 'Maybe we can get some kids to sing with us.' So we get some kids, who were very nice and very professional, and we put them in skeleton makeup. So we have these kids. And we had not played this song as much as a band would like. We did our best in the time we had. But the song is kind of unconventional. It's not like a lot of things you were hearing on the radio at the time. So I'm not sure it translated the first time we played it. We just kind of made our way through this thing. And I remember at the time, I think the sentiment on the song from the general public was just kind of like, 'What was that? There are these kids in skeleton makeup, and we're in all these uniforms, and I can't really understand the song.' And that was the vibe I got. People were like, 'Oh, that was great.' But I was like, 'I don't think this translated.'"

That inauspicious debut was like a galaxy far, far away from thirteen years later, when the reunited band closed their triumphant first show in eight years with the song before thousands of screaming fans singing every last word in unbridled ecstasy at LA's Shrine Auditorium.

"We did know that we wanted to play 'Black Parade' last. We felt like this is the one to end with. This song will probably heighten the last of everyone's energy, but all they have left for the end of the night, whatever is left from the whole show is gonna go into 'Black Parade,' because it did become this kind of anthem," Way says. "And it does do something, once it really kicks in. I can kind of barely control myself once it kicks in, especially back in the day when I'd be so energized by what we were doing, I would fall over, convulse, or whatever else. But something happens when that ring-out happens at the end of the introduction that has gotten very intense, and then there's that moment of quiet, and then there's just that drum fill and there's something about that that energizes absolutely everybody in the room, including the band."

So how did the song's place in the world change so dramatically in the thirteen years from when it was released to the band's first reunion show? Going back to the writing, Way says he knew the band was onto something special from the outset.

"Yes, we knew it was special. The song actually had started as this song called 'The Five of Us Are Dying,' which is like a riff on an old *Twilight Zone* episode title. It was these chords we really liked, it was a striving kind of a punk song. But as the concept of the record started to come together, we realized it was a special song, but I started to realize during the actual tracking of the album, that there was no song that introduced or encapsulated some of the concepts on the record in that way," he recalls. "There was definitely stuff that was capturing certain conceptual elements, like hell, and being raised Catholic, and mothers, and it had a lot of stuff, there's like a war theme. But there was no 'Black Parade' song, and I had known that that's what I wanted to call the album."

As Way reflects on the recording of the song, it wasn't always a smooth process until the idea of the parade came into play. "It was actually a really hard song to record, because we were, in some ways, so used to the original version that when it came time to start changing things, it was just very difficult. And nobody knew if it was the right direction, and things like that," he says. "But then I started to envision this parade, and so then I wanted to bring in certain elements. I would ask Bob [Bryar], 'Play a marching beat.' But when it really started to come together is when I had this melody in my head, this piano melody, and I was like, 'Bob, I think I have the way I want to start this song.' So when the actual tracking happened is when it started to come together and really flesh out, as sections got added and things changed."

The final pieces of the song eventually fell into place because of where they were recording, historic Eldorado Studios in Burbank, where everyone from Alice in Chains, Red Hot Chili Peppers, and David Byrne to Herbie Hancock, Jewel, and Jane's Addiction have recorded.

"We were at Eldorado, which we liked. And there was a piano in this side room, so I went over there with Bob and he sat at the piano and I basically sung out all the notes, 'cause I can't really play piano. I could cheat my way through some stuff and I could write parts. I sit with keyboards actually a lot right now, and I can write parts, but at the time especially I just had very little experience with playing keys. So I sung it out and Bob just followed it, and then we had that, and then it started to come together," Way says. "Then we put the vocal on. And so then we built this introduction for this song with a marching beat and a parade beat. And it really set the stage, I think, for the song to become something much greater than just, let's say, a driving punk song. Since we were envisioning this kind of parade that comes for you, like death, the song just got more ambitious and grew and grew, and then just started throwing a ton of stuff on it. I know when Chris Lord-Alge mixed the song, at the time he had told us it was the most tracks he had ever had to mix in a song. I'm sure in the years later something beat that but, at the time, it was the most tracks he had ever mixed."

It probably didn't hurt the song's eventual place in history that it had one of the most popular songs ever, Queen's "Bohemian Rhapsody," as a huge inspiration for the complexity of "Black Parade."

"'Bohemian Rhapsody' was always an influence on this song. Just these big, sweeping section changes and things like that. But at the same time, I had realized when we were working on it, you can't remake 'Bohemian Rhapsody.' You could be a little inspired by it, but we can't try to do that," Way says. "What I like to do sometimes in music is to be inspired by things from the past, but what you present people is something that has a really positive familiarity to it. Almost like something that gives you the feeling of something without having to be like it. And that was one of those songs that we realized, 'Well, we're not gonna copy 'Bohemian Rhapsody.' But we're going to make this big, epic thing like 'Bohemian Rhapsody,' in that way. I like a degree of familiarity. I like a degree of bringing people music that triggers something in them, like an old feeling from the past, without completely ripping the thing off. To me, these are little nods, and that's why it almost becomes like putting Easter eggs in the song. These little nods to things, that when you put them in the song, you're almost saying like, 'We really like Queen.' We're really trying to honor stuff, and that's why Queen, the [Smashing] Pumpkins, have been a big influence. I still explore Pumpkins stuff and explore those themes and sonic landscapes of theirs."

While "Welcome to the Black Parade" was influenced by the likes of Queen and the Smashing Pumpkins, the song feels totally original and unique and speaks to the emo generation singularly because it's told through Way's very personal and literary bent. It is his story.

"For me, a theme that I explore sometimes, and I definitely explored lyrically in 'Black Parade,' was the triumph of the human spirit over darkness, over tragedy. Self-actualization has been a theme in a lot of the lyrics that I've written, kind of becoming what you're supposed to become, evolving, changing, cocooning into your next form," Way says. "And I just talked about this with Billy [Corgan] in that interview we did. I asked him if he thought that rock was a transformative thing, specifically rock. And he said, 'Yes. I think it's transformative.' So the triumph of the human spirit over darkness was something that was kind of built into the DNA of the band from the beginning. The self-actualization, the triumph of the spirit and things like that, getting through really hard things."

The song was impacted by Way's relationship with his grandmother, whom he had written about previously. "Obviously, I lost my grandmother before we started writing *Revenge* and that loss really impacted me, because she had been the person to sit with me and teach me how to draw or make me go to the piano with her. And she would play and she would make me sing along with her and stuff, so that we had a really amazing relationship," he says. "So it was that loss and wanting to get over that loss and kind of triumph over that loss to kind of make her proud that drove me in songs like 'Helena.'"

Going back to that Shrine show, "Welcome to the Black Parade" is, as Way says, an obvious closer. It is one of the most powerful live songs of this century, an explosive, joyous anthem that lifts crowds from a thousand fans to one hundred thousand in a feverish sing-along.

Because of the song's complex nature, it took a minute for the track to secure its place as a live anthem. Way recalls that it didn't happen until partway through the tour for the album.

"Unless my memory is faulty, I don't think we got to really play that live for people until the official Black Parade Tour, unless I'm wrong. Because it was the first single, and because it kind of encapsulated the concept and themes of the record, and because of the lyric being kind of meaningful to us, we'd have to play it for mostly these taped performances. So we didn't really get to get it in front of a live crowd for some time," he says. "And then during the official kind of Black Parade Tour in arenas, this thing started to happen, I noticed, when we would play it live, and it was almost like the whole audience started to kind of sing all those words, which can happen to a number of songs. But it started to feel like it had this power and that big kind of intense intro leading into just this full-on-force, wall-of-sound, driving kind of punk thing generally just made all of us and the audience lose our minds and get a little bit out of control."

Once the song eventually took its rightful place as a centerpiece of the live set, it became as immediately recognizable to fans as any live song out there, thanks to the piano.

"I've learned this in recent years, one of the most interesting things about the song is that it's identifiable by one single note. That G note on the piano," Way says. "And recently, I saw Andrew Lloyd Webber did a video where he discussed this. He was sitting at a piano, and I think he played a bit of *Phantom of the Opera*. He's like, 'It's one thing to kind of know a song by its opening melody. And it's another thing to be able to identify a song by one note.' He played the G note and everybody was like, 'Oh, that's "Black Parade."' That's something pretty crazy about the song, is just hearing that single piano. And that's something that we saw live when we would play it. We'd have to wait for it to kind of get quiet enough for people to hear it, 'cause a lot of times the audience was competing with our actual sound. Like Mexico City, for example, I think the audience was louder than us. So we would have to let enough air, enough quiet happen, and then we'd just play that G note, and then it was crazy. Just that single note."

That familiarity, triumph of the spirit, and punk wall of sound Way and his bandmates conveyed in the song made the deeply personal and uplifting track one of the most unlikely sports anthems of all time, at least for a short period, when the LA Kings hockey team adopted the song, a flattering choice, even for New Jersey Devils fans, as Way recalls.

"That was interesting. We were very flattered by that. They started to use 'Black Parade' and we had heard about it. That was kind of the first usage I really remember. And that was many years later, obviously, so yeah, the Kings, they're doing this thing and we got put in an awkward situation because we're all from Jersey," he says, laughing. "Our team is the Devils, and they were like, 'Will you guys come and play "Black Parade" for the Kings? This is like their song and they're gonna win. This is a really big moment.' And we were kind of like, 'I don't think we can.' Because even though some of us live here now, we're Jersey boys."

Over the more than fifteen years since the song has been part of the world, it has had several honors, maybe none bigger or crazier for Way than the Rock & Roll Hall of Fame selecting the track as one of the five hundred songs that shaped rock 'n' roll.

It was listed right between Naughty by Nature's "O.P.P." and Mott The Hoople's "All the Young Dudes." "Dude, 'All the Young Dudes,' that was a really big, influential song to me. There's times for sure where I was trying to write things that had that energy," Way says.

The same way he was moved by songs like "All the Young Dudes" and "Bohemian Rhapsody," which he calls the "greatest rock song of all time for a number of reasons," "Welcome to the Black Parade" has had that effect on others, like Ariana, a woman living in Argentina who was woken up by her mother with "Welcome to the Black Parade" every birthday.

During the years My Chem was on hiatus, Way was consciously careful not to buy into the hype of the song, as he wanted to be away from social media and fanfare.

"So let's talk about what happens when you release a song. Once you put something out, it is no longer yours, and it is no longer your story. For example, all I listened to for five months was *Black Parade* while we were making it. It was the music that excited me more than anything, it was the music that moved me more than anything else, it was what I was all about. And then we released it, and then at that point, with all the songs we had done, I let go of it, and I was just like, 'It's no longer ours. This is the world's. And they're going to do whatever they want with it,'" he says. "So I don't listen anymore to that stuff, and the only time I hear it is when we play it live. Of course, I've heard it on the radio and stuff, and Lindsey, my wife, is so sweet, and she gets so excited when she hears My Chemical Romance on the radio, especially 'Black Parade.' But yeah, so I don't listen to these things anymore. Years ago, I had realized that I needed to disconnect from opinion, so I don't read reviews; I don't look at that stuff. I like to keep my channel as an output channel, not an input. And I think that really keeps the art pure."

As much as Way stayed off social media and away from reviews, he wasn't isolated from the world as the band's popularity grew exponentially during the several years they were broken up. He still heard from fans how the band's music and that song, in particular, kept growing in popularity with fans.

"In the universe of My Chemical Romance, with My Chemical Romance's fans and playing these tours and headlining these shows, it had started to become an anthem pretty quickly. But in terms of it becoming an anthem for the world or a larger audience or people outside that universe, that did take some time," Way says. "Even though I don't kind of engage with social media, I don't read reviews, I don't read anything, I would hear the little stories about it, or I would meet somebody that would say, 'Oh, "Black Parade" is my song.' And yeah, in the years the band broke up, I would hear little things and then I started to get this sense that this is kind of an anthem. It's a big song to people. Yeah, that did take some time, but I would hear little stories."

That the song has become the band's signature anthem is particularly meaningful for Way because, as he thinks back to writing it in LA all those years ago, he points out it is very much a song that combines all elements and voices from My Chemical Romance.

"One little detail I just want to make sure is in there, is that despite bringing certain sections into it or altering things, or at least bringing the suggestion of altering things, that song, like a lot of My Chem stuff, was really this collaborative experience," he says. "We're just in this kind of haunted house together, kind of becoming slowly depressed and withdrawn and isolated from the world outside. I don't remember us ever leaving this house, here at the Paramour [the LA mansion where the album was recorded]. It became a dark place. And just being in there and kind of jamming this idea together and just kind of playing it together and getting the original bones of the song, that was really collaborative."

When Way looks back now he sees, once again, that feeling of overcoming adversity in the song, which is so much of why it has become a modern-day anthem.

"There's darkness in the world. And I think overcoming that darkness, that darkness externally and internally, is a beautiful thing. It's a challenging thing, but it is beautiful if you can do that, if you can kind of triumph over that. So that's a theme that's definitely in 'Black Parade.'"

NOTES

✦

THE BEACH BOYS
"GOD ONLY KNOWS"

1.   Steve Baltin, "Q&A: Glass Animals' Dave Bayley on the Band's Surprise Hit, 'Heat Waves,' Returning to the Stage and More," *Forbes*, May 3, 2021, https://www.forbes.com/sites/stevebaltin/2021/05/03/qa-glass-animals-dave-bayley-on-the-bands-surprise-hit-heat-waves-returning-to-the-stage-and-more/?sh=43d45817506c.
2.   "Sir Paul McCartney Cries When He Hears God Only Knows," LondonNet, September 19, 2007, https://www.londonnet.co.uk/entertainment/sir-paul-mccartney-cries-when-he-hears-god-only-knows/.
3.   "Quotes," BrianWilson.com, accessed March 10, 2022, https://www.brianwilson.com/quotes.
4.   "Quotes."
5.   "Quotes."

NEIL DIAMOND
"SWEET CAROLINE"

1.   Ian Browne, "How 'Sweet Caroline' Became a Fenway Hit," MLB.com, January 21, 2021, https://www.mlb.com/news/sweet-caroline-red-sox-fenway-park-history.

BOB MARLEY
"ONE LOVE/PEOPLE GET READY"

1.   Steve Baltin, "Neil Young, Carlos Santana, Joan Baez and More Pick the Greatest Protest Song of All Time," *Forbes*, March 23, 2018, https://www.forbes.com/sites/stevebaltin/2018/03/23/neil-young-carlos-santana-joan-baez-and-more-pick-the-greatest-protest-song-of-all-time/?sh=3fee9ee77641.
2.   Steve Baltin, "Ben and Jerry's Celebrate Bob Marley with One Love Flavor," *Forbes*, May 30, 2017, https://www.forbes.com/sites/stevebaltin/2017/05/30/ben-and-jerrys-celebrate-bob-marley-with-one-love-flavor/?sh=265c2ac759bc.

EARTH, WIND & FIRE
"SEPTEMBER"

1. Dan Charnas, "The Song That Never Ends: Why Earth, Wind & Fire's 'September' Sustains," NPR News, September 19, 2014, https://www.wbur.org/npr/349621429/the-song-that-never-ends-why-earth-wind-fires-september-sustains.

CHIC
"LE FREAK"

1. "National Recording Registry Reaches 500," Library of Congress, March 21, 2018, https://www.loc.gov/item/prn-18-028/national-recording-registry-reaches-500/2018-03-21/.

TOTO
"AFRICA"

1. Rae Paoletta, "What's the Best Song, According to Science?" Gizmodo, July 17, 2017, https://gizmodo.com/whats-the-best-song-according-to-science-1796927071.

U2
"ONE"

1. Dorian Lynskey, "Why U2's One Is the Ultimate Anthem," BBC Culture, November 17, 2021, https://www.bbc.com/culture/article/20211117-why-u2s-one-is-the-ultimate-anthem.
2. Steve Baltin, "Sunday Conversation: U2's Adam Clayton on 20 Years of 'All That You Can't Leave Behind,' Springsteen, Growing Older in Music and More," *Forbes*, December 6, 2020, https://www.forbes.com/sites/stevebaltin/2020/12/06/sunday-conversation-u2s-adam-clayton-on-20-years-of-all-that-you-cant-leave-behind-springsteen-growing-older-in-music-and-more/?sh=25a9a9e552ee.

ACKNOWLEDGMENTS ✦

When you do a book with interviews of twenty-nine of the biggest acts in music it takes a mountain of support to schedule all of these artists.

Thanks to every artist who participated in *Anthems We Love* and every person who helped set up these interviews and believed in the book early on. Jeff Jampol and the team at JAM, Inc, Luke Burland, Bobbie Gale, Meg McLean Corso, Lauren Albanese, Katie Diamond, Fran DeFeo, Kristen Foster, Sujata Murthy, Jean Sievers, Jonathan Wolfson, Michael Jensen, Marilyn Duckworth-Davis, Rona Menashe, Kelly Kettering, Ryan DeMarti, Victoria Varela, James Adams and Leila Hebden, Larry Ciancia, Steve Hart, Karen Wiessen, Aliza Rabinoff, Mark Young, Steve Karas and Keith Hagan, Dana Erickson and everyone at Grandstand, and, lastly, a special thank you to the late Lisa Roy, who helped secure interviews with Linda Ronstadt and TLC, but tragically passed away New Year's Eve 2021. Lisa, you were always a great supporter and you are missed.

Then there is my support system. Monica Molinaro, the perfect plus-one for all of our adventures over the years; Michelle and Joey Chavez, Jen DeSisto, Adam and Seana Chavez; the amazing Katie Deatrick Trimble, Robert Friedson, Dani Miskell, Bill Crandall, Aimee Lay, Michelle Cano, Nick and Amy Noonan, Jen Potter, Fay Aiyana Grant and Ben Grant, Claire Hunter, Lauren Daddis, Jessica Perlman, Jessica Madia, Stephanie Lauber,

Katrina Kaufman, Alex Rosen, Ann Ingold, Stephanie Belcher, Lauren Novik Black and Cody Black, Liz Wiltshire, Kristin Wymard, Seshmila Jay, Liberty Cordova, Jayden Fleener, Shivani Southwick, Heather LaRose, Ophelia Zuniga, and Chak and Diggs for keeping me company while writing. And especially Alli Delavan, for help with transcribing and being there all these years.

The industry support team who were excited and encouraging about the book—John Sykes, Marcie Allen Van Mol, Peter Katsis, Jonathan Shank, Darryl Dunn, Ted Stryker, Heather Parry, Wayne Kamemoto, Liza Aristizabal-Hesse, Jackie Barrie, Ronilyn Reilly.

All the early readers—Dia Frampton, Paola Mondragon, Ivana Steelman, Tatiana Steelman, Rebecca Aaron, and of course Cameron Crowe, the first person to read the book all the way through. Thanks for the kind words to keep me going.

This book was inspired by my being a proud music geek. So special thanks to my concert-going companions in my early formative days. Louis Matza, Jasmine Brinton, Brett Robbins, Bob Kaufman, Nicole Rongo Sheehan, and my cousin Sandra Nieves, who was with me at the first shows where I got stoned. My dad, Bruce Baltin, for my first Springsteen shows, for taking me to see the Stones at twelve years old and especially the US Festival as a thirteen- and fourteen-year-old. So much of my passion for music I can remember coming from sitting as a little kid looking through my parents' record collection.

My extended family—Susie and Harold Jacobs; Sam, Francois, Eliza, and Alex Jouin; Victoria, John, Russell, James, and Molly Dougherty; Mark, Roberta, and Aimee Baltin; Hanna and Fiona Jacobs.

Finally thanks to everyone at Harper Horizon—Andrea Fleck-Nisbet, John Andrade, Amanda Bauch, and Meaghan

Porter. And to those not at Harper but who were instrumental in this book getting done—J. Reid Hunter, without whom this book never sees the light of day; Joseph Llanes, for the great headshots and great hangs always; all of the photographers, like Anton Corbijn, who provided the photos, and Jamie Bucherer for all the help with the photos.

STEVE BALTIN is a Southern California–based music journalist/author/host. He hosts the podcast *My Turning Point* and the streaming series *Riffing With,* and has written for *Rolling Stone,* the *Los Angeles Times,* and countless other publications, as well as the book *From the Inside: Linkin Park's* Meteora.